WITHDRAWN

RACING

THE ULTIMATE MOTORSPORTS ENCYCLOPEDIA

RACING
THE ULTIMATE MOTORSPORTS ENCYCLOPEDIA

CLIVE GIFFORD

KINGFISHER
BOSTON

KINGFISHER

a Houghton Mifflin Company imprint
222 Berkeley Street
Boston, Massachusetts 02116
www.houghtonmifflinbooks.com

First published in 2006
10 9 8 7 6 5 4 3 2 1
1TR/0706/PROSP/CLSN/170GLS/C

Editorial manager Russell Mclean
Editor Simon Mugford
Coordinating editor Caitlin Doyle
Art editor Claire Legemah
Imaging and photo manipulation Nick Harris
Illustrations by Julian Baker, Nick Harris
Poster designed by Malcolm Parchment
Consultant Matt Salisbury
DTP manager Nicky Studdart
DTP operator Claire Cessford
Senior production controller Jessamy Oldfield
Picture research manager Cee Weston-Baker
Picture researchers Su Alexander, Clive Gifford
Indexer Alan Thatcher
Additional U.S. research assistance: Branden
  Reeves

LIBRARY OF CONGRESS CATALOGING-IN-PUBLICATION
  DATA
Gifford, Clive.
  The Kingfisher racing encyclopedia / Clive
Gifford. — 1st ed.
    p. cm.
  Includes bibliographical references and index.
1. Motorsports—Encyclopedias. I. Kingfisher (Firm).
  II. Title.
GV1019.2.G54 2006
796.72092—dc22

Printed in China

Note to readers The Web site addresses listed in this
book are correct at the time of going to print.
However, due to the ever-changing nature of the
Internet, Web site addresses and content can change.
Web sites can contain links that are unsuitable for
children. The publisher cannot be held responsible for
changes in Web site addresses or content or for
information obtained through third-party Web sites.
We strongly advise that Internet searches are
supervised by an adult.

CONTENTS

THE NEED FOR SPEED

People have always been fascinated by pushing the boundaries, whether testing themselves against others or their environment. The invention of motor vehicles in the 1800s introduced a new thrill—a combination of humans and machines that tested technology and individual skills like they never had been tested before. As competitions and vehicles developed, the exciting world of motorsports was born.

100 YEARS OF RACING

Today, drivers and riders compete in an incredibly diverse range of events and racing classes over widely varying distances. Racing, both on two wheels and on four, is conducted on roads, on racing circuits, and on tracks, and off-road, it is done over mud, desert, ice, and other tough terrain. Vehicles range in power from tiny pocket bikes and mini karts

to tough Superbikes, Formula One (F1) cars, and dragsters. There is one underlying similarity for every class of motorsports—at its heart is a need for speed.

In 1894, the French newspaper *Le Petit Journal* organized the Concours des Voitures sans Chevaux (the contest for horseless carriages). In that contest, vehicles raced from Paris to Rouen and back; the record speed was 11.7mph (18.8km/h). In 2004—100 years later—Brazilian motorcycle rider Alex Barros set the MotoGP speed record of 212.66mph (343km/h) on a Honda, while his fellow countryman Antonio Pizzonia reached 229.34mph (369.9km/h) in a Williams F1 car. Even more amazing, the fastest of the Top Fuel dragsters can race along a drag strip at a breathtaking 310mph (500km/h). Only a few people will have the chance to experience such devastatingly high speeds firsthand. Millions more maintain their fascination by following motor racing in its many forms all over the world as spectators.

▶▶ *At the 2005 Brazilian Grand Prix, Fernando Alonso celebrates being crowned Formula One's youngest-ever world champion.*

▼ *Flames blast out of William Costes' Yamaha during a practice for the Chinese round of the World Endurance Championship in 2004.*

▶ *Sweden's Mattias Ekström competes in the Race of Champions, in which rally drivers and Formula One drivers go head-to-head.*

THE EXPLOSION OF MOTORSPORTS

From its small beginnings, motor racing has boomed to become one of the world's leading spectator sports. It is also a huge business—with hundreds of millions of dollars spent on competitions, vehicle and engine development, circuits, major race teams, media coverage, and sponsorship. Leading drivers, riders, and vehicles are world famous and loved by the media and sponsors. Most of the world's leading motorsports are administered by the *Fédération Internationale de l'Automobile* (known as the FIA). Formed in 1904, it organized the first recognized World Championship for racing in 1950—the competition known today as the Formula One World Championship. Currently, membership of the FIA is made up of more than 210 national organizations. The FIA helps oversee a large number of racing events throughout the world, including the World Rally Championship (WRC), World Touring Car Championship (WTCC), and World Karting Championship. A similar organization for motorcycle racing, the *Fédération Internationale de Motocyclisme*

(FIM), was also founded in 1904. It governs many motorcycling competitions, including the MotoGP and World Superbike championships. In the U.S., the Sports Car Club of America (SCCA) runs several events, including the Trans-Am Series for road-racing sports cars. Other leading championships, such as NASCAR and the Indy Racing League, are also run independent from the FIA.

▲ A pack of riders takes a curve in a 250cc motocross race—a thrilling combination of speed, mud, and noisy high-octane action.

▲ 2003 Champ Car champion Paul Tracy pushes his car to the limit in the heat in Long Beach, California, in 2005.

EARLY DAYS

True motor racing began in 1895 with the daunting 730-mile (1,178-km) -long Paris–Bordeaux–Paris race. Emile Levassor was the first one across the line, with a time of 48 hours, 48 minutes. French cars dominated the early events, which followed the pattern of racing from one city or town to another. With the arrival of closed-circuit racing, rallies, and track racing, vehicles from Italy, Germany, the U.S., and Great Britain rose to prominence.

▲ *Camille Jenatzy, the winner of the 1903 Gordon Bennett Cup, in his Mercedes. Capable of 74mph (120km/h), the car was one of the fastest of its day.*

CITY TO CITY

The first major race across national borders was the 1898 Paris–Amsterdam–Paris event, won by Fernand Charron. By the beginning of the 1900s, huge crowds would gather, fascinated by these amazing racing machines. As traffic increased and car speeds rose toward 62mph (100km/h), safety concerns grew. These concerns came to a head in 1903, when the French government banned road racing but then relented for the 1903 Paris–Madrid event. The race only lasted for one day, as the deaths of 15 people—both drivers and spectators—saw it stopped. Open-road racing almost completely ended in France, but it flourished elsewhere, especially in Italy, where the Coppa Florio and the Targa Florio were first run in 1900 and 1906 respectively.

FROM GORDON BENNETT TO GRAND PRIX

In France in 1900, the owner of the *New York Herald* newspaper, James Gordon Bennett, Jr., founded the Gordon Bennett Cup—the first truly international competition. For the first time, there were strict rules and a formula based on the weight of the cars. In 1906, the Herkommer Trophy—arguably the forerunner of modern rallying—was held in Germany, and the first-ever Grand Prix (GP) took place in France, close to the town of Le Mans. Meanwhile, in the U.S., William K. Vanderbilt II had founded the Vanderbilt Cup. Held between 1904 and 1916, it was North America's first major motor race.

▼ *British racing driver John Cobb takes one of the notoriously steep banks of the Brooklands track as he competes in the Broadcast Trophy Handicap.*

CLOSED CIRCUITS AND TRACKS

In 1898, the first known closed-circuit race (in which a race is run around a loop of public road that has been closed off from regular traffic) was held in France. The Course de Périgueux featured enormous "laps" that were around 90 miles (145km) long. This form of racing became very popular in most of Europe. Racing on shorter closed circuits and dirt tracks was more common in the U.S. For example, at the Indiana State Fair dirt track in 1903, Barney Oldfield became the first racer to complete a circular mile (1.6km) in less than one minute. The U.S.'s longest-surviving major racetrack—the Indianapolis Motor Speedway—opened in 1909. Two years later, it held the first Indy 500, one of motorsports' greatest races.

The very first oval circuit built specifically for racing opened in Great Britain in 1907, where racing on roads was illegal. Funded by Hugh Locke-King, Brooklands was a monster of a circuit, with a track that was more than 98 feet (30m) wide and banked corners that rose to 33 feet (10m). It was the scene of many motor-racing milestones, including Percy Lambert's 1913 record, when, in a 4.5-liter-engined Talbot, he became the first person to cover 100 miles (160km) in less than one hour.

RACING CONDITIONS

Early racing cars were incredibly basic. Many did not have brakes, the tires offered little grip, safety helmets were unheard of, and the usually open-topped cars offered little protection to the drivers in the event of a crash. The routes, whether closed or open, were often deadly, with trees and dust obscuring the view and hiding lethal ruts and pits in the road. Cars were often unreliable, occasionally forcing drivers to adopt unusual racing techniques. During the 1899 Tour de France race, for example, Fernand Charron lost all of the forward gears on his Panhard close to Le Mans. He drove backward for around 25 miles (40km) to complete the stage!

▲ Until the mid-1920s, drivers were often accompanied by a mechanic, who could perform repairs while on the move—from topping up water and oil to replacing an engine valve or a tire. Here, Arthur Duray's mechanic struggles with a tire during the 1906 Vanderbilt Cup.

◄◄ The thrills of racing at the Indianapolis Motor Speedway are shown by the cheering crowds in this advertising poster—one of the first for the circuit.

▼ Georges Boillot and his mechanic reach 74mph (120km/h) in their Lion-Peugeot car during a speed trial at Brooklands in 1911.

GOLDEN ERAS

The period between World War I and World War II is considered by many to be the first golden era of motorsports. While it lacked some of the charisma of the period between the wars, the decade after the end of World War II was also a vital period, as it saw the early organization and founding of many of today's leading motorsports competitions.

▲ *Three legends pose for a photo after a race at Silverstone in 1950: (from left to right) Alberto Ascari, Juan Manuel Fangio, and Guiseppe Farina.*

A GOLDEN AGE

Despite the devastation that World War I caused in Europe, the need for excitement and entertainment remained, and motorsports reemerged. In 1921, the French Grand Prix was held in Le Mans, where, two years later, the famous Le Mans 24 Hours endurance race ran for the first time. This was a true test of a car's stamina, reliability, as well as its headlights, which were then still in their early stages. Other nations organized Grand Prix races, including Spain (1923), Belgium (1925), Germany (1926), Great Britain

(1926), Czechoslovakia (1930), and the legendary race at Monaco (1929). As the Great Depression made its impact, the "Formula Libre" era began in 1928, which saw many rules abandoned and a greater variety of cars welcomed into events. Racing cars were developing fast, from the Fiat 805.405 (one of the first cars to be tested in a wind tunnel) to Benz's streamlined, teardrop-shaped Tropfenwagen. By the 1930s, the Grand Prix cars driven by legends such as Louis Chiron, Rudi Caracciola, and Tazio Nuvolari, had developed into slim single-seaters with fearsomely powerful engines. French manufacturers, such as Bugatti and Delage, and Italian firms, including Maserati and Alfa Romeo, led the way until the arrival of the formidable German "Silver Arrows" built by Mercedes and Auto Union in the mid-1930s (see p. 130).

ON TRACK

In mainland Great Britain, where motor racing on public roads was still banned, racing took place on grass tracks and on specially constructed circuits such as Brooklands (until its closure in 1939). In 1924, France built its own competitor to Brooklands, the 1.6-mile (2.6-km) -long Montlhéry Autodrome, at the then huge cost of $930,000. It was used for the French Grand Prix in 1925 and throughout the 1930s, as well as for saloon car racing. In the U.S., large numbers of dirt-track circuits appeared. These

◄ *After World War I, Grand Prix racing began again in 1921. The U.S.'s Jimmy Murphy scored a surprise win at the French GP, driving this Duesenberg car.*

were followed in the early 1920s and 1930s by tracks made out of wooden boards. Consisting of thousands of wooden planks, they provided a fast but short-lived racing surface for some important races, particularly between the Duesenberg cars and those of Harry Miller (see p. 128).

GETTING ORGANIZED

The years immediately after World War II saw rapid development in many areas of motorsports, particularly in the formation of organizations and major competitions that still survive to this day. As hot-rod enthusiasts returned to racing on strips and salt lake flats in California, the National Hot Rod Association (NHRA) was formed in 1951. Motorcycling had already held its first World Speedway Championship at Wembley Stadium in London, England, in 1936, and further international competitions resumed soon after the war. The first Motocross des Nations was held in the Netherlands in 1947; two years later, the most prestigious motorcycling competition of all, the Road Racing World Championship Grand Prix, started with five classes—125cc, 250cc, 350cc, 500cc, and a sidecar class. Grand Prix car racing resumed in 1947, with the Swiss Grand Prix (Swiss GP), one of four Grand Prix that was held that

year. Three years later, the Formula One World Championship began with a race at Silverstone in Great Britain. From this point on—and despite many disputes over rules, entries, and withdrawals—F1 grew in strength and popularity. It was helped throughout the 1950s by an amazing number of truly great drivers, such as Juan Manuel Fangio, Stirling Moss, and Alberto Ascari, who produced compelling races in F1, as well as in sports, endurance, and road races such as Italy's Mille Miglia.

AMERICAN RACING

In the U.S., stock car racing was growing in popularity. Developed in the South, where modified cars had been used for transporting illegal alcohol during the Prohibitioon, races were organized sporadically until the race promoter Bill France, Sr. held races that led to the formation of the National Association for Stock Car Auto Racing (NASCAR) in 1948. The first NASCAR "Strictly Stock" race was held at the Charlotte Speedway in North Carolina on June 19, 1949. Three years before, the AAA National Championship, along with its most famous race, the Indy 500, had resumed, with Ted Horn winning three titles in a row. And in 1956, Art Ingels, an employee of the leading U.S. race car designers Kurtis-Kraft, built the first kart out of scrap metal, pioneering a low-cost racing class that would be adopted by thousands of drivers around the world.

▲ Peter Collins, driving a Sunbeam Talbot Alpine, takes a mountainside bend during the 1954 Alpine Rally, one year after the European Drivers' Championship had started.

▼ Cars roar past a pileup at a 99-mile (160-km) -long stock-car race at Daytona Speedway, Florida, in 1953.

▲ Brian Ducker's sidecar partner performs a daredevil move on their way to winning a 1936 race at Great Britain's Brands Hatch circuit.

TRIUMPH AND TRAGEDY

Only the best drivers and riders can win major motorsports races. The rewards are fame, fortune, excitement, and glory—but the threat of danger is never far away. Motor racing is a sport, but it is not a game. It is a potentially lethal activity, but this risk is part of its appeal for many drivers and spectators.

▲ *Ferrari's Formula One world champion Michael Schumacher leaps up in the air after winning the San Marino GP in 2004.*

THE REWARDS

Motorsports offer many rewards—from the thrill of high-speed racing to the glory of the winner's podium. Many types of racing can offer professional competitors an excellent lifestyle. In the wealthiest classes, such as NASCAR and Formula One, the drivers are multimillionaires. Race winnings alone can total more than $6 million for a NASCAR season, while Michael Schumacher's F1 contract with Ferrari is believed to pay him around $35 million per season. In addition, the best and most famous drivers can see their income soar through sponsorship, merchandizing, and media opportunities.

HIGH-RISK RACING

Motor racing has always involved a high level of risk. In 1898, the Marquis de Montaignac and his mechanic were killed during the Course de Périgueux. They were the first fatalities of motor racing. Early races were deadly, with no crash helmets, few safety features, and unmapped routes. Spectators would wander onto roads, causing accidents. Only the relatively low speeds kept the death tolls from being much higher. But, as reliability, brakes, and circuits improved, the risks changed, with speeds hitting 124mph (200km/h) in the 1930s. By 1971, it was estimated that 840 racing drivers had died.

◄ *Incredibly, Geoff Bodine suffered only a broken wrist and ankle after this NASCAR Craftsman Truck Series crash at Daytona, Florida, in 2000.*

▲ *MotoGP rider Alex Barros of Brazil crashes his Yamaha at high speed during the Australian GP in October 2005. He escaped with only minor cuts and bruises.*

▲ *British driver Dan Wheldon kisses the famous BorgWarner trophy after winning the Indy 500 in 2005.*

▶▶ *At Le Mans in 1955, Pierre Levegh corners in a Mercedes 300SLR shortly before his tragic crash. The race was continued in order to prevent spectators from leaving, which would have blocked all access roads for the ambulances.*

Being a skillful, experienced driver has never guaranteed protection against accidents and injuries, as was proven by the deaths of Jim Clark in 1968, Henri Toivonen in 1986, and Ayrton Senna in 1994. Marshall Teague, Neil Bonnet, and Dale Earnhardt are just three of the NASCAR greats who have been killed at Daytona—a circuit that has seen 28 drivers lose their lives since 1959. Many spectators have also perished over the years. In 1928, Emilio Materassi crashed into the crowd at Monza, Italy, killing himself and 27 spectators. At the same circuit 33 years later, Wolfgang von Trips and 14 spectators were killed—an event that saw Ferrari withdraw from racing for the rest of the season. Forty-one drivers have been killed at the Indianapolis Motor Speedway during racing, qualifying, or testing. An additional 23 spectators, mechanics, or track officials have also died there.

A DEADLY SEASON

The tragic deaths of U.S. sprint-car star Mike Nazaruk, Indianapolis legend Bill Vukovich, and the great Alberto Ascari all occurred during the 1955 season. The worst accident of all in that tragic year came during the Le Mans 24 Hours. Pierre Levegh's Mercedes flew off the track, killing himself and more than 80 spectators and injuring more than 100. Racing was then banned in France, Spain, Switzerland, and Mexico (in Switzerland, the ban remains to this day). Mercedes withdrew from motorsports and did not return until the 1980s.

THE RISK REMAINS

Greater protection for drivers, better marshaling and fire precautions, safety barriers, and improved cars and tracks have made some types of racing safer. Formula One has not had a fatality since the death of Ayrton Senna in 1994 (see pp. 72–73). But serious risks still remain, and a number of drivers, including Mika Hakkinen and Michael Schumacher, have since suffered severe injuries. The start of this century has already seen several tragedies, including the deaths of MotoGP star Daijiro Kato in 2003, codriver Michael Park at the 2005 Wales Rally Great Britain, and two F1 marshals (at the 2000 Italian GP and the 2001 Australian GP), killed by flying debris from crashes. Another marshal, this time at the 2005 Isle of Man TT, died as she crossed the circuit and was hit by rider Gus Scott, who also died.

DALE EARNHARDT

By 2001, Dale Earnhardt had done it all in NASCAR, winning seven championships (a record shared with Richard Petty) and more than 70 races. In 1998, after 20 years of trying, he won the one major race to have eluded him—the Daytona 500. At the 2001 race, Earnhardt took the lead on lap 27. It was the 23rd time he had led a Daytona 500, but going into the final lap, he was in third place behind Michael Waltrip and his own son, Dale Earnhardt, Jr. Heading into turn four, Earnhardt's rear bumper touched the front bumper of Sterling Marlin's car, sending the number 3 car down and then up the track, where it hit the wall. Earnhardt died on impact, and U.S. racing mourned the loss of one of its finest and most popular drivers.

▲ NASCAR legend Dale Earnhardt, in his famous black number 3 Chevrolet, hugs an inside line as he races ahead of Jeff Gordon (24) and Sterling Marlin (40) at the Daytona 500 in 2001.

At the age of 47, Dale Earnhardt celebrates his long-awaited win at the Daytona 500 in 1998.

OPEN-WHEEL RACING

Different types of motorsports are called classes. Open-wheel racing is one of the most popular groups of classes. It involves single-seater race cars that have their wheels outside of (rather than covered by) the car's body. Run on tracks and road circuits, open-wheel racing includes Formula One, Indy racing, and Champ Cars. Below we take a look at some of the other open-wheel classes.

▼ *Swedish legend Ronnie Peterson drives a March to the Formula Two title in 1971. In the same year, he was the runner-up in the F1 World Championship.*

CHANGING CLASSES

Various open-wheel competitions have come and gone. Those no longer in existence include Formula Junior, which ran from 1958 to 1964, and Formula Opel. In Australia, Formula Brabham gave way to Formula Holden and is now known as "Formula 4,000 powered by Holden." Formula Two (F2) began in 1948, and for many years, it attracted the top Formula One drivers on weekends, when there were no F1 races. The exact formula for F2 cars changed over the years, with 750cc, 1,000cc, 1.6-liter, and two-liter engines all permitted at different times. There was no Formula Two World Championship, but many famous racers, including Jacky Ickx and Ronnie Peterson, won the F2 European Championship. In 1985, F2 was replaced by Formula 3,000 (F3,000), which was intended to be a cheaper form of racing than F2, despite using three-liter (3,000cc) engines. Notable graduates from Formula 3,000 include Rubens Barrichello, Mika Hakkinen, Juan Pablo Montoya (the 1998 F3,000 champion), and Sebastien Bourdais (F3,000 champion in 2002 and Champ Cars champion in 2004 and 2005). But as Formula 3,000 costs rose, entry numbers dwindled. In 2005, GP2 replaced it, with the aim of offering a fairer test of drivers' skills.

▼ *John Miller and Declan Quigley make contact during a Formula Ford race at Brands Hatch, U.K., in 2005.*

Competitors all have to use the same chassis, engine, and tires. The engine generates around 70 percent of the power of an F1 engine and, in order to cut costs, can only be rebuilt after 2,480 miles (4,000km) of action. GP2 also features a two-race weekend format, with the positions of the top eight finishers on Saturday being reversed on the starting grid for the shorter race on Sunday. This livens up the competition, as drivers fight for the eighth place, which will be pole position the next day.

FEEDER CHAMPIONSHIPS

Many formulas are seen as "feeder" competitions for bigger, more powerful, and more expensive classes of racing. Aspiring young drivers take part in these competitions, hoping to attract attention and sponsorship with their promising

▲ Marco Andretti, the grandson of the great Mario Andretti, won three races in the 2005 Infiniti Pro Series—at St. Petersburg (shown here), Indianapolis, and Sonoma—before moving up to IRL.

performances. Formula Three (F3) is one of a number of classes that have traditionally provided experience for drivers with Formula One potential. It began in 1950 and developed out of 500cc-engined cars that were built by Cooper. Especially popular in Europe, South America, and Australasia, national and international F3 competitions paved the way for such stars as Stirling Moss in the 1950s, Jackie Stewart and Emerson Fittipaldi in the 1960s, Ayrton Senna in the 1980s, and, more recently, Jenson Button and Nelson Piquet, Jr. Today's F3 cars have wings, a monocoque body, and two-liter, four-cylinder engines that can achieve speeds of 161mph (260km/h). The climax of many F3 seasons is the Macau GP, held at the Guia Circuit in China since 1983 (the first winner was Ayrton Senna).

In North America the Indy Pro Series (which began in 2002 as the Infiniti Pro Series), acts as a feeder competition for the Indy Racing League (IRL). The Toyota Atlantic Championship, which

has been running for more than 30 years, has produced some IRL champions, such as Dan Wheldon and Sam Hornish, Jr., but many of its race winners go on to be Champ Car stars—Bobby Rahal, Gilles Villeneuve, Jimmy Vasser, and Paul Tracy, for example.

ENTRY-LEVEL RACING

There are a number of lower or junior formulas, giving young racers their first taste of open-wheel circuit action. Formula Vee racing remains a real low-cost entry point. Based on the Volkswagen (VW) Beetle, a Vee car costs between $18,000 and $26,000, while a season's racing totals from $7,500 to $11,000. Speeds average only 81–93mph (130–150km/h), but the competition is stiff and the racing is intense. Formula Vee is popular in North America, Great Britain, Germany, Australia, and New Zealand. Formula Ford and Ford 1,600 are steps up in terms of speed, cost, and power, but they are still considered to be a starting point for young racers. Very popular at an amateur level in many countries, Formula Ford has very distinctive cars, with no wings and with their wheels a long distance from their narrow bodies. But the cars are no wimps: the best of them have top speeds of more than 124mph (200km/h) and can accelerate from 0 to 60mph (0–100km/h) in under five seconds. Many championships exist for this class of vehicle. The U.K. Formula Ford Championship, for example, celebrated its 40th birthday in 2007.

◄◄ Olivier Panis of France races at the 1990 Formula Three Macau GP. Over the years, a number of its winners have moved up to compete in Formula One.

▼ Germany's Michael Ammermüller drives for Arden International in the 2006 GP2 Series—the championship that replaced F3,000 in 2005.

CHAMP CARS AND INDY RACING LEAGUE

▲ Canadian Paul Tracy crosses the finish line in second position at the Grand Prix of Long Beach, during the 2005 Champ Car World Series.

Championship, or Champ, Car racing has been a popular, mostly North American, class of exciting and dramatic open-wheel racing for decades. Following many changes and a lot of controversy, there are now two major competitions—the Indy Racing League (IRL) and the Champ Car World Series.

THE CART YEARS

Championship racing in the U.S. was first run by the American Automobile Association (AAA) and then by the United States Automobile Club (USAC). From 1979, the premier event was the Championship Auto Racing Teams (CART) championship. For its first 15 years, CART saw American drivers of the caliber of Mario Andretti, Al Unser, Jr., Bobby Rahal, and Rick Mears dominate; the only nonAmericans to win the championship were Emerson Fittipaldi in 1989 and Nigel Mansell in 1993. The jewel in the

▶▶ *Roberto Guerrero of Colombia competes in the 1992 CART Series. Guerrero held the Indy 500 qualifying speed record of 232mph (374km/h) from 1992 until 1996.*

crown of this class of racing was the Indianapolis 500—the longest-running major race in the world. But a dispute between CART and the owners of the Indianapolis Motor Speedway led to a split in 1996. The Indy Racing League (IRL) was formed as a challenger to CART. Following the split, CART remained the dominant championship, so it came as a shock when the organization went bankrupt in 2003. Its replacement the following season was the Champ Car World Series.

SIMILARITIES . . .

There are notable similarities between the vehicles and racing of the two series. Compared to a Formula One vehicle, Champ Cars and IndyCars are heavier. An F1 car typically weighs around 1,320 lbs. (600kg) with its driver. An IndyCar is around 1,540 lbs. (700kg) without fuel or its driver, and a Champ Car is 1,562 lbs., or 710kg, (1,538 lbs., or 699kg, at oval circuits) without its driver. In 2006, following the withdrawal of engine suppliers Toyota and Chevrolet from the IRL, both series only use one engine supplier. Both Champ and IndyCars use methanol as a fuel—F1 cars use racing gasoline—and both begin their races from a rolling start. The six-person pit crew must stay behind the pit wall until the car arrives. Champ Cars and IndyCars feature a specially shaped underside that allows them to generate ground effect (see p. 129); the semiautomatic transmissions that are found in F1 are forbidden.

. . . AND DIFFERENCES

The two series have very different circuits, and this affects the strategy, car setup, and driving tactics. The Indy Racing League is predominantly an oval circuit series. It used oval circuits exclusively until 2005, when it added three road circuits to its schedule, including the famous Watkins Glen International track outside of New York City. Out of the 14 venues in the 2004 Champ Car season, six were permanent road circuits, including the Laguna Seca and Elkhart Lake circuits. Six more were exciting temporary road circuits laid out in the streets of cities such as Montreal, Denver, and Cleveland. Only two, in Milwaukee and Las Vegas, were ovals.

POINTS AND RACES

Champ Cars awards points for the first 20 finishers—first place receiving 31, second place 27, third place 25, and so on in two-point drops until tenth place and then one-point drops until 20th place. In contrast, IRL awards 50 points to the

winner, 40 to second, and 35 to third, with points diminishing down to ten for any car finishing between 25th and 33rd. IRL awards a three-point bonus to the car that led the most laps, compared to Champ Cars' one. Champ Cars offers several other bonus points, including one to each driver who leads the race for at least one lap. Both series are based in the U.S., but Champ Cars has more races abroad than the IRL. The 15-race Champ Car season for 2006 included three races in Canada, two in Mexico, and single races on Queensland's Gold Coast in Australia and at Ansan in South Korea. Champ Cars' roll call of drivers is even more international. In the 2005 season, won by France's Sebastien Bourdais, the top ten drivers included three Canadians, two Americans, a Spaniard, a Mexican, a Briton, and a German. Although mostly an American series, the IRL also attracts drivers from around the world. Its champions include Brazil's Tony Kanaan (2004), New Zealander Scott Dixon (2003), and Swede Kenny Bräck (1998). Japan's Kosuke Matsuura was the IRL Rookie of the Year in 2004. Great Britain's Dan Wheldon won that award the previous year and fulfilled his promise by becoming the IRL champion in 2005.

▲ *Dan Wheldon (number 26), Jeff Bucknam (44), and Felipe Giaffone (top) race in the 2005 Indianapolis 500— the biggest event of the Indy Racing League.*

▲ *British driver Katherine Legge during testing for the PKV Racing team at Sebring, Florida, in December 2005. The following year Legge drove for PKV in the Champ Car World Series.*

◀◀ *The BorgWarner trophy, awarded to the winner of the Indy 500, is studded with the faces of every winner from 1911 to the present day.*

FORMULA ONE

The biggest, most glamorous, and costliest class of motor racing, Formula One (F1) has millions of fans from all over the world. The teams drive highly-advanced, superfast cars that compete over a series of Grand Prix races to secure the sought after World Drivers' and World Constructors' Championships.

▲ Ferrari's Rubens Barrichello of Brazil sprays himself with champagne. He had just won the 2002 European GP at Nürburgring, Germany.

WINNING FORMULA

Today's Formula One race is made up of the least number of laps of the circuit that make a total distance of more than 189 miles (305km). Most races last around 90 minutes; some take as long as two hours. Between 20 and 24 cars take part—two cars per team—participating in practice and then qualifying for as high of a position as possible on the starting grid. The race begins from a standing, not rolling, start. An hour and a half of high-speed, high-stakes racing follows, as drivers and teams plot their best path to victory. Strategy and pit-stop timings can make or break them.

▲ Peter Gethin in action in 1971—the year that he won the Italian GP with the fastest average speed ever (150mph, or 242.6km/h).

THE PINNACLE

Formula One is the most advanced form of open-wheel racing. With their massive budgets, teams can lure the best of driving and engineering talent to produce and race incredible vehicles. F1 cars are lightweight—they weigh around 1,320 lbs. (600kg, or half the weight of a family saloon car)—but they develop as much as 900 horsepower. This means that the vehicles can accelerate at the start and out of bends at lightning speeds: from 0 to 60mph (0–100km/h) in under three seconds. F1 cars do not attain average speeds as high as those of IndyCars racing on a fast oval circuit such as Indianapolis. This is because Formula One cars have to be set up for constant changes in pace

on the track—chicanes and hairpin bends, for example, that dramatically slow down their progress. In addition, the FIA has insisted on track changes and car modifications to slow down cars for safety reasons. Nevertheless, Formula One cars still race at ferocious speeds. In 2005, during the Italian GP, Kimi Räikkönen averaged more than 158mph (254km/h) completing a lap of the Monza track, which includes a number of sub-81mph (130km/h) bends. Down long straights, cars frequently exceed 198mph (320km/h) before they have to start braking and cornering. At the 1998 German GP, David Coulthard was recorded racing at 221mph (356.5km/h) down a straight. Such a performance costs a lot of money, and Formula One teams have the largest budgets of all of the motorsports. In 2004, McLaren spent almost $38 million on vehicle development, and that is just the tip of the iceberg. Yearly engine budgets may be almost four times that amount, while testing may set a team back up to $52 million per season. Many teams have entered Formula One over the years, some with huge budgets, but between 1984 and 2005 only four outfits—McLaren, Williams, Ferrari, and Benetton (which was bought by Renault)—won the World Championship.

▲ Michael Schumacher, Fernando Alonso, and Kimi Räikkönen are caricatured at the 2005 Chinese GP, Shanghai—one of the newest races in F1.

WORLDWIDE APPEAL

Formula One has global appeal, partially because of the speed and technical prowess of the vehicles, but also because of its glamour, history, and outstanding drivers. Many successful drivers from other major classes of motorsports have tried and failed at Formula One: Mario Andretti's world drivers' title in 1978 was a notable exception. F1 teams are based in Europe, but their personnel come from around the world. Drivers for 2006 included Colombia's Juan Pablo Montoya, Australian Mark Webber, Takuma Sato of Japan, and the U.S.'s Scott Speed. Past world champions have not only come from Europe, but also from Australia, South Africa, Canada,

Argentina, and Brazil. F1 is a true world sport with a global set of fans. Hundreds of millions of fans tune in for televised races; thousands more sell out circuits, in spite of high ticket prices. Formula One's racing calendar has worldwide appeal too. Recently, it introduced new races in the Middle East and Asia. The first three Grand Prix races of 2006 were in Bahrain, Malaysia, and Australia, while the last three were in China, Japan, and Brazil. Turkey is another new arrival; its Istanbul Park Circuit made its Formula One debut in 2005.

▲ The checkered flag signals the end of the race. It is waved at the winner and held still for all of the other finishers. Here, McLaren's Räikkönen wins the 2003 Malaysian GP.

◄ Stefan Johansson's Ferrari blazes along the track at the 1985 Monaco GP. Of the 26 cars that entered, six did not qualify; nine, including Johansson's, retired during the race.

THE GRAND PRIZE

Grand Prix (meaning grand prize) races were first held in France more than 100 years ago. After World War II, an international Grand Prix championship was set up by the FIA. Formula One officially began in May 1950 at Silverstone, U.K., with the launch of the World Drivers' Championship. The World Constructors' Championship was added in 1958: the Vanwall team was its first winner, and Ferrari is currently the most successful team, with 14 constructors' titles by the end of 2005. Point scoring has changed over the years. In the past, fractions of points were awarded if drivers shared the same car. Today, the top eight finishers at each Grand Prix score points, with the winner receiving ten points, the runner-up eight points, third place six points, and every successive place receiving one less point. If a race is abandoned before it has run three quarters of its distance, the points are split in half. The points that are gained count toward the World Drivers' Championship and also the Constructors' Championship for the teams. Occasionally, a team wins "by a mile," as in 1988, when McLaren won 15 out of 16 races and scored 199 points (134 more than any other team). At other times, a team may win the constructors' title without securing the drivers' crown—in 1999, for example, Ferrari was the leading constructor, but McLaren's Mika Hakkinen was the top driver.

TESTING, TESTING . . .

The F1 calendar has grown from six races in 1950 to 19 in 2006. Races are held from March to October, but the short off-season is hardly a vacation. It is an exceptionally busy time for the teams as they integrate new drivers and develop and test new cars. Testing is a complicated and expensive business. In 2006, *F1 Racing* magazine estimated that McLaren spent more than $16 million per season on wind tunnel testing alone. On the track, teams organize extensive testing sessions. Toyota's winter testing session in 2005–2006 saw them complete more than 8,500 laps of circuits. Each lap costs more than $1,300 in consumable items such as brake pads, fuel, and tires. The buildup intensifies as the opening race approaches, with teams having to deal with massive fan and media interest.

◄◄ *From left to right, F1 legends Ayrton Senna, Alain Prost, Nigel Mansell, and Nelson Piquet in 1986.*

▲ *Ahead of the 2006 season, Pedro de la Rosa tests the new McLaren MP4-21 near Valencia, Spain.*

▼ *Renault's Fernando Alonso (left) is chased by Toyota's Jarno Trulli (right) and Ferrari's Michael Schumacher (left, behind) during the 2005 French GP.*

PRACTICE AND QUALIFYING

An F1 race is traditionally held on a Sunday, but the action starts a few days before when teams arrive at the circuit and begin their free practice (usually on the Friday, except in Monaco, where it is held on the Thursday). Qualifying takes place on Saturday and sees short, frenetic bursts of action as the teams send their drivers out onto the track to post as fast of a lap time as possible. Results during qualifying determine the lineup on the starting grid. Cars are positioned in rows of two across on a straight section of the track, with the fastest-qualifying driver in pole position—the place on the front row of the grid that is considered to be the optimum starting point. Like many other aspects of F1, the rules regarding qualifying have changed often over the years. In the past, for example, there was the notorious 107 percent rule. In most cases, this meant that any car that did not record a qualifying time within 107 percent of the pole-position time could not race and went in the record books as "DNQ" (did not qualify). In 2006, a knockout system was introduced. After the first 15-minute qualifying session, the six slowest cars are pulled out of qualifying and occupy the last six places on the starting grid. After a second 15-minute qualifying period, the same thing happens to another six cars, which will occupy the starting grid positions 11 to 16. The final ten cars battle it out over a third and final 20-minute qualifying session, but with one twist—they must attempt to qualify with the amount of fuel that they wish to start the actual race with. After qualifying, the fuel levels are checked, and fuel is topped up for the race. This system gives teams the option of different strategies. For example, if a team gambles on having an emptier, faster car for qualifying, it may start from a better position, but it will need an extra or longer pit stop to refuel during the race.

▲ *The Italian Jarno Trulli, driving for Toyota, suffers from engine failure during preseason F1 testing at the Circuit de Catalunya, Barcelona, Spain, in January 2006.*

LIGHTS OUT . . . GO!

Given the high level of interest and the incredible amount of finance that is invested in each team, it is no surprise that the pressure mounts in the lead-up to an F1 Grand Prix. Drivers are the ones who are under the most intense scrutiny. On the big day, they cannot focus solely on the race: they also have numerous media and sponsor commitments, a driver briefing, a parade around the track, and any final team orders and discussions. The cars that they race in will have been locked up by 6.30 P.M. the evening before in the *parc fermé*—a secure area of the paddock. Only minor adjustments are allowed to the setup of the car between qualifying and the actual race. Half an hour before the race starts, cars are allowed to go out onto the track to perform a few last reconnaissance laps. Then it is time for the formation lap, which ends with the cars lining up on the grid in their starting positions. All eyes turn to the starting light system. Five pairs of lights switch on at one-second intervals. When these lights go out, the race begins, and the cars surge forward.

▲ A McLaren crew member holds the pit board at the 2005 Brazilian GP. It displays Juan Pablo Montoya's position (first), the number of laps left (18), and the gap, in seconds, to the two cars closest behind.

▼ F1 pits are crammed with crew who perform superfast pit stops—some can refuel and change tires in under seven seconds.

FORMULA ONE FLAGS

| Danger ahead: slow down and do not overtake. | All clear: resume racing. | Slow-moving vehicle on the track. | A faster car behind is trying to overtake and lap. | Driver has broken the rules: return to the pits. | Car has a problem: return to the pits. | Slippery track surface ahead. | Practice, qualifying, or the race has been stopped. |

VITAL SIGNS

As an F1 driver thunders around a circuit, striving to make the perfect racing line, he or she constantly monitors the positions of their rivals and their own car's performance. Each time they pass their pit lane, they check the information on the pit board that is held up by their team. The driver must also keep an eye out for colored flags (see below, left), which are displayed by marshals. Each part, or sector, of track has its own flag marshals and a supervising sector marshal who is in charge. In particular, an F1 driver dreads seeing a black flag displayed along with his or her car number. It tells the driver that they must enter the pits to be penalized or disqualified for breaking the rules.

When conditions become dangerous or a major accident occurs, the safety car may appear on the track. It provides another warning system and limits the speed of competing cars as they follow along behind it in order around the circuit until the danger has passed and racing can resume.

▲ *Lella Lombardi is the only female F1 driver to have scored championship points (half a point in the 1975 Spanish GP). She was the second woman to qualify for a GP; the first was Maria Teresa de Filippis in 1958.*

F1 FEATS

More than six decades of F1 racing have seen many magnificent champions and challengers engage in tremendous action and set some amazing records. Considered to be the finest racer of the early era, Juan Manuel Fangio remains the oldest-ever world champion (at the time of his fifth win in 1957, he was 47). In 2005, F1 crowned its youngest world champion, 24-year-old Fernando Alonso. By the end of the 2005 season, Michael Schumacher held many of Formula One's records, including most points (1,248), most podium finishes (142), and most wins (84). Other notable F1 records include the most pole positions in one season (Nigel Mansell took 14 out of 16 in 1992), and the oldest driver to win a race (Luigi Fagioli was 53 years old when he won the 1951 French GP).

▲ *Safety marshals push a Sauber (top) and a Jordan off the circuit after a multicar accident on lap one of the 2002 Australian GP.*

▼ *Ralf Schumacher lands in the gravel after a jump over Cristiano da Matta during the 2004 European GP. The crash knocked both drivers out of the race.*

A1 GRAND PRIX SERIES

The idea of a complementary competition to Formula One is not new. Between 1964 and 1969, for instance, the Tasman Series for Formula One cars raced in the winter in Australia and New Zealand. However, the A1 Grand Prix (A1GP) series is a radical development: it has a different race format to F1, and competitors represent different nations, rather than different constructors.

▲ *Round ten of the 2005–2006 A1GP season took place at Laguna Seca, California, in March 2006. Team Mexico driver Salvador Duran won both the sprint and feature races.*

▲ *Khalil Beschir (Team Lebanon) rolls his car over at the first-ever A1GP at Brands Hatch, Great Britain, in September 2005.*

THE WORLD CUP OF MOTORSPORTS

The brainchild of Sheikh Maktoum of Dubai, the A1GP series was developed to take high-speed racing all over the world and was sanctioned by the FIA in 2005. The A1GP organization sells franchises to national teams: cars are painted in their country's colors and can only be driven by drivers of that nationality. Twenty-five teams took part in the first season (2005–2006). Each franchise costs between $16 and $53 million and was priced according to the wealth and population of each particular country. Major racing powers, such as France, Italy, Germany, Great Britain, and the U.S. were present, but so were countries that were less well-known in motorsports such as Pakistan, Lebanon, Malaysia, and Indonesia. With such populous nations as India, China, Russia, and the U.S. involved, the organizers were

able to boast that the teams on the track in the first season represented around 80 percent of the world's population. The 11 rounds were also spread out worldwide, with the first at Brands Hatch, U.K., in September 2005, followed by races in Germany, Portugal, Australia, Malaysia, the United Arab Emirates, South Africa, Indonesia, Mexico, and the U.S. The final round was held at China's Shanghai International Circuit, in April 2006.

LEVEL PLAYING FIELD

The aim of A1GP is to give every team a fair chance—as well as drivers' skills, it tests the teams' organization and tactics, rather than just finances and resources. Expensive track testing is only allowed on official days. While gear ratios and suspension settings can be altered, no major modifications are permitted to the engine. Each A1GP chassis is built with identical features by the race car manufacturer Lola. It comes with a 3.4-liter engine produced by Zytek that generates 520 horsepower and offers a top speed of just over 186mph (300km/h). The cars are 12–31mph (20–50km/h) slower than F1 vehicles, but their aerodynamic setup encourages them to race closer together so that spectators see more of the overtaking. This is assisted by a PowerBoost button, as in Champ Cars, which gives drivers a burst of extra engine horsepower—30 horsepower

▶▶ *Alexandre Prémat drives the Team France car in Durban, South Africa, in January 2006. The car is red, white, and blue—the colors of the French flag. France won the title ahead of Switzerland and Great Britain.*

to be precise—for a few seconds. This button can be used up to four times during the sprint race and eight times during the feature race (see below). Exciting images of the action can be taken from four different cameras, which are mounted on the cars. With their huge 135-liter fuel tanks, A1GP cars can run a race without refueling, but they still have to make one pit stop per race to change all four wheels and tires. A1GP pit crews are much smaller than they are in Formula One—only ten people are allowed in total, and only five are allowed over the pit wall to perform the pit stop.

THE A1 EXPERIENCE

The A1GP hopes to attract new audiences to motorsports, as crowds come to support their national entry. There is extensive media coverage, and tickets are cheaper than they are for Formula One events. The lure of many famous names helps too: team leaders, or principals, include former F1 world champions John Surtees (U.K.),

Niki Lauda (Austria), Alan Jones (Australia), and Emerson Fittipaldi (Brazil), the latter with Brazilian soccer star Ronaldo as coteam leader. Practice and qualifying take place on the Friday and Saturday of a race weekend, and qualifying features an exciting system in which each car must attempt a fastest lap time in each of the four 15-minute sessions. A car's fastest two laps are added together to determine its grid position for the first race. On the Sunday there are two points-scoring races— a sprint race and a feature race. The finishing positions in the sprint race determine the starting grid for the feature race. The sprint race lasts around 30 minutes and has a rolling start, like IndyCar racing. The feature race has a standing start and lasts around one hour. Ten points are awarded to the winner of each race, with each position below that receiving one less point. In addition, there is an extra point awarded for the team that records the fastest lap time over the two races. At the Malaysian A1GP, for instance, Alexandre Prémat (Team France) scooped up all 21 points available, and his team went on to win the inaugural championship.

▲ A1GP principals— and former F1 champions— Emerson Fittipaldi, Niki Lauda, Alan Jones, John Surtees, and Keke Rosberg at the A1GP Dubai, United Arab Emirates, in December 2005.

◄◄ Tengyi Jiang (Team China) waits in his garage at Eastern Creek Raceway, Australia. His car featured a painted dragon.

▼ Stephen Simpson (Team South Africa) at Brands Hatch, U.K., in September 2005. Team Brazil won both races that day.

NASCAR

The National Association for Stock Car Auto Racing (NASCAR) was set up by Bill France, Sr. in 1948. It is now the U.S.'s favorite of all motorsports, with more than 75 million fans. They cheer to top speeds of more than 198mph (320km/h), four-across racing, daring overtaking moves, frequent changes of lead, and exceptionally close finishes.

ON THE TRACK

Early stock cars were regular saloon cars, but they were tuned for extra speed on the racetrack. Today's NASCAR vehicles are capable of generating more than 750 horsepower from their eight-cylinder engines. They mostly race on oval or modified oval tracks, although two Nextel Cup races are held on road circuits—the Infineon (formerly Sears Point) Raceway and the famous Watkins Glen

International track. The length of a NASCAR circuit varies greatly, from the 2,778-foot (847m) Martinsville Speedway to the longest and fastest circuit, the Talladega Superspeedway. The record average speed over an entire race at this 2.65-mile (4.28-km) -long circuit is a remarkable 188mph (303km/h). The number at the end of a NASCAR race name can signify laps, miles, or kilometers.

A WHOLE LOTTA RACES

NASCAR sanctions many different series of race competitions, but the big three are the Busch Series, the Craftsman Truck Series, and, at the pinnacle, the Nextel Cup. Previously known as the Grand National an the Winston Cup, the Nextel sets more than 40 of the best racers against each other in a 36-round competition.

▲ *The Petty Enterprises pit crew works on John Andretti's car at the 2003 Auto Club 500. Air guns are used to loosen and tighten the wheel nuts, while the car is refueled from two fuel cans, each one weighing 75 lbs. (34kg).*

▶ *Two NASCAR champions— four-time winner Jeff Gordon (left) and Matt Kenseth—lead at the start of the first Dickies 500, held at the superfast Texas Motor Speedway in November 2005.*

▲ *Bobby Labonte (47) and Todd Kluever (50) collide during a 2005 Craftsman Truck race. Labonte is a NASCAR veteran, winning the 1991 Busch Series and the 2000 Nextel Cup, while Kluever was a rookie in 2005.*

The Busch Series is the second tier of NASCAR. Many drivers, including Dale Earnhardt, Jr. and the 2002 champion, Greg Biffle, successfully step up from the Busch Series to the Nextel Cup. The Craftsman Truck Series developed out of demonstration racing and the 1995 Supertruck Series. Drivers race modified pickup trucks over distances of between 149 and 248 miles (240–400km). It, too, has seen drivers such as Kyle and Kurt Busch move into Nextel Cup racing, while also providing places for veteran NASCAR racers who drop down from the top division.

IT'S THE PITS!

With a fuel consumption of approximately one mile (1.6km) per liter, top NASCAR vehicles are not run for economy—they are tuned for gut-wrenching speed and performance. Fuel tanks empty fast, and several times in a typical race, drivers leave the track to refuel, change tires, and make repairs. The position of a driver's stall in the pit lane is determined during qualifying, with the pole-position driver having first choice. A pit team of seven leaps over the wall and works in a fast, well-rehearsed routine. A tire change and refueling stop can be completed in less than 15 seconds. In the pit lane, NASCAR inspectors each patrol two stalls. They assess whether the pit stop has been carried out according to the rules. Crews that jump over the wall too early, have more than seven over the wall, use more than two air guns, or have no one catching the fuel overflow are liable to a 15-second penalty in the pits before being allowed to rejoin the race.

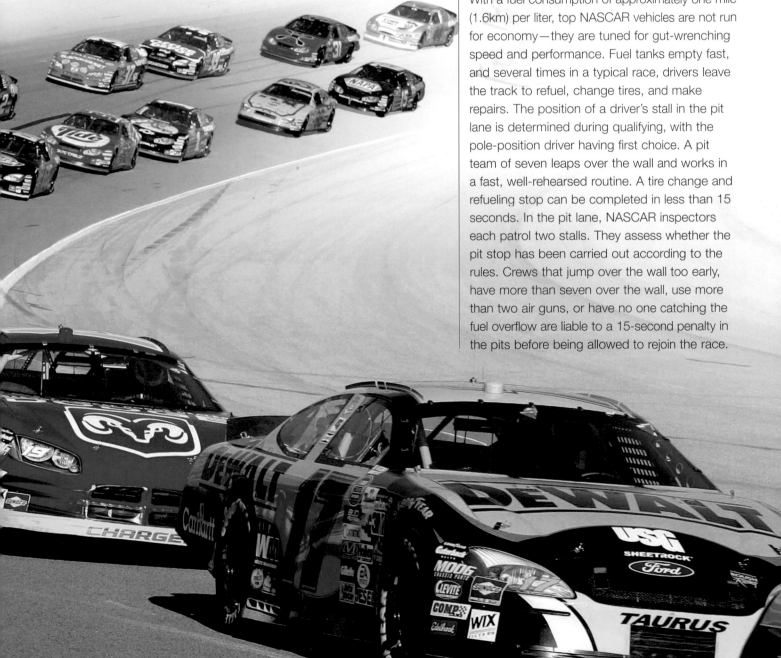

▲ As Dale Earnhardt prepares for the start of the 1999 Save Mart 300, the steel frame and window webbing of his Chevrolet are clearly visible.

▼ A NASCAR official prepares to attach a speed-limiting restrictor plate to the engine of a car at the 2002 Daytona 500.

A NASCAR UNCOVERED

Although NASCAR was originally a competition for stock cars (models that can be purchased from a showroom), the vehicles that are raced today only bear a surface resemblance to their road-bound cousins. The 2006 Nextel Cup was contested by three makes of vehicles—Chevrolet, Ford, and Dodge. Aside from some body panels, each vehicle is custom-built around a strong tubular steel frame. This is divided into a sturdy central roll cage, a rear section known as a rear clip, and a front clip section that is designed to crumple on impact so that a lot of the force of a crash is absorbed and safely channeled around the car. Nextel Cup cars must weigh a minimum of 3,392 lbs. (1,542kg) and use a high-performance V8 engine that generates more than 750 horsepower without restrictor plates (see below). This can propel the car at speeds of more than 198mph (320km/h). In contrast, the transmission is much less advanced—it has four speeds and is manually operated, like in a regular car. Fuel is supplied by an 83-liter tank, known as a fuel cell, which has a tough plastic inner layer and a steel outer layer. A NASCAR vehicle races on treadless tires known as slicks, and teams change tires up to six times per race. A NASCAR has no doors or side mirrors, and its hood is fastened securely with hood pins. Certain pieces of technology that are found in other classes are outlawed in NASCAR, including onboard computers and traction control devices. All cars have a transmitter called a transponder, however, which measures a car's lap time and sends that information to a remote computer.

SAFETY FEATURES

In 1952, Tim Flock won a NASCAR Modified-Sportsman race at Daytona Beach, but he was disqualified because his roll cage was made out of wood instead of metal. Compared to some other major racing series, NASCAR was slow to adopt certain safety measures until the deaths of Dale Earnhardt and three other drivers in 2000 and 2001. Today's NASCAR, however, is packed with safety features. These include an in-car fire extinguisher, window webbing that prevents a driver's arms from flailing outside of the car in the event of a crash, and windshields that are made out of shatterproof Lexan (see p. 70). Each car only contains one seat and is made to measure out of carbon fiber or titanium and aluminum. This is covered by a thin layer of foam and fitted with a strong and secure racing harness. NASCAR drivers wear full fireproof clothing, a helmet, and, since 2001, a HANS (Head And Neck Support) safety device (see p. 70). On the fastest circuits, the superspeedways of Talladega and Daytona (home of NASCAR's most famous race, the Daytona 500), an engine-power-limiting device called a restrictor plate is attached to all cars. This limits the amount of air and fuel that can enter the engine's cylinders, cutting back each car's top speed. There is, however, continuing debate over their effectiveness. Critics argue that they result in more "bunched-up" racing, which some people fear will lead to the "big one"—a major multicar accident.

▶ Roush Racing's Greg Biffle attempts to qualify for the 2005 Dodge/Save Mart 350 at Infineon Raceway in California. He went on to finish as the runner-up in the 2005 Nextel Cup.

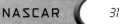

▲ Sparks fly from Steve Park's badly damaged Chevrolet during the 2003 Chevy Rock & Roll 400, held at the Richmond International Raceway in Virginia.

RULE ENFORCERS

The spiritual home of NASCAR is the state of North Carolina, where around three quarters of the teams are based. The NASCAR organization, however, has its headquarters in Daytona, Florida. Under the chairmanship of three different generations of the France family, it has governed the sport's rules. These rules are long and complex, requiring dozens of trackside officials to ensure that they are followed by each driver and team. Most visible are the race officials who display flags to tell the drivers about certain situations. These can be general, such as the red flag that stops the race, or more specific, such as the black flag that tells a certain driver to leave the track and head to the pits. This can be because of a fault with the car or so that the driver can be penalized for breaking a race rule. The yellow flag instructs all drivers to slow down, as the race is under caution due to an accident, oil spill, or dangerous weather conditions. Under a yellow flag, cars may not change their race position and must follow the safety car, known as the pace car, around the track until the situation changes. When the cars are driving under caution, the field tends to bunch up. This benefits a car that is far from the lead but on the same lap as the leaders. For a car with a half-lap lead, however, it can prove to be frustrating, as the following cars can close up the distance behind it.

▲ Four-across racing is part of the thrill of NASCAR. Here, (from bottom) Tony Stewart, Johnny Sauter, Ricky Rudd, and Casey Mears battle for position at the 2004 Aaron's 499.

RACE DAY

A NASCAR race weekend features sessions of practice and then qualifying to determine each car's place on the grid, which can contain a maximum of 43 vehicles. Only the Daytona 500 is different, with qualifying for pole and second place occuring the weekend before. The rest of the competitors then battle it out in two 124-mile (200-km) -long races four days later. Qualifying times determine the starting positions, but NASCAR is so competitive, that even racers

▲ Sterling Marlin (left) goes wheel-to-wheel with Kasey Kahne during the Subway 500 Nextel Cup race at Martinsville Speedway, Virginia, in October 2005. Marlin went out of the race on lap 370, but he still banked more than $90,000 in race winnings.

►► NASCAR vehicles do not have doors, so drivers pull themselves in through the windows. Here, Bill Lester climbs into his Dodge Craftsman truck in 2003. Three years later, Lester became the first African-American to qualify for a Nextel Cup race since 1986.

many rows back on the grid may still have a chance of victory as their race speed and other drivers' mistakes and mechanical problems give them opportunities to advance up the field. In 2001 and 2002, for example, both Michael Waltrip and Ward Burton started from a low 19th position, yet they went on to win the Daytona 500, while in 1978, Bobby Allison won the race from 33rd on the grid.

Make no mistake, NASCAR racing is fast and furious. Drivers charge around the track, facing the ever-present threat of fast-moving traffic and unforgiving outer walls. As well as bravery, they need intense concentration and stamina in order to last the three to four hours it takes to complete a 496-mile (800km) race. NASCAR fans cheer at frequent changes of lead and constant shifts in positions. At the Talladega Superspeedway in 2001, for example, 26 different drivers held the lead throughout the race.

Strategy is a vital part of many NASCAR races. Teams figure out the precise timing of pit stops, while a team member called the spotter— who has a vantage point above the track— informs the driver of their position and the

positions of their rivals. Drivers must carefully choose when to draft (see p. 66), when to overtake, when to drive within their own and their car's abilities, and when to gamble and take a high-speed risk. Racing saps a driver's stamina and the workings of the car, and many races see dramatic shifts in positions during the closing laps. Victory is rarely guaranteed until the lead car has crossed the finish line.

POINTS AND PRIZES

NASCAR's point-scoring system appears to be complex, but essentially, drivers earn points for their final race position and any laps that they have led. 180 points are awarded to the race winner and 170 to the runner-up. Points then drop by five per position to sixth, by four points from seventh to 11th, and by three points after that. A driver also receives five points for each lap that they lead during the race. A further five points are awarded to the driver who led the most laps.

The race winner, therefore, may not actually gain the most points from an event. Some drivers and teams employ a conservative racing strategy, trying to avoid DNFs ("did not finish") and focusing on accumulating points. In 2003, for example, Matt Kenseth became the champion through consistent driving that led to 25 top-ten finishes, although he only won one race. The previous year he had won five races, yet he only finished eighth in the championship. From 2004, the Nextel Cup points system was altered, partially in order to attract greater television coverage. After 26 races, the top ten drivers and any others within 400 points of the leader earn a place in the "Chase for the Championship"—a ten-race sequence that determines the ultimate champion. Today, money that is awarded for points-scoring finishes, plus bonuses for various achievements, including fastest lap or most laps led, can really add up over a Nextel Cup season. In 1949, the race winnings of NASCAR champion Red Byron equalled $5,800. In 2005, Nextel Cup champion Tony Stewart earned $6,987,530 from race winnings.

NASCAR's FUTURE

Since the 1990s, media coverage of NASCAR and television and live audience numbers have rocketed, making it by far the most popular class of racing in the U.S. In 2005, more than 35 million people watched the Daytona 500 broadcast live on television. Later that year, NASCAR signed a television rights deal with Fox that was worth an estimated $4,480 million. Yet the sport still faces certain problems—from concerns about safety to teams going out of business, or racing part-time due to the high costs or a failure to attract enough sponsors. The NASCAR organization is not standing still, however. Foreign manufacturers are being courted to boost competition—the 2007 season is expected to see the arrival of Toyota's Camry vehicle in the Nextel Cup (its Tundra vehicles already compete in the Craftsman Truck Series). NASCAR recently unveiled its Car of Tomorrow—a new type of vehicle that is due to race in many events in 2007. The car has numerous new safety features, including a larger front bumper, a more central driver position to help protect the driver against side impacts, and an exhaust system that keeps the heat farther away from the driver.

▲ Jimmie Johnson celebrates his victory at the 2006 Daytona 500—the opening race of the NASCAR season.

▲ Jeff Burton tests the Car of Tomorrow in 2005. Among its safety features is a windshield that slopes less than on a traditional NASCAR, increasing drag and reducing its top speed.

◄ Matt Kenseth is pressured by Tony Stewart during the Dickies 500 race in November 2005. Stewart finished fifth and went on to win the 2005 championship.

TOURING AND SPORTS CARS

Touring car racing is a popular form of circuit racing that features racing versions of standard road cars—usually four-seater sedans or saloons or two-seater coupés. These road cars offer exciting and close racing. Sports car racing is for more exotic vehicles—usually two-seater sports cars or supercars with fearsome incredible power and slick handling.

▲ *A Ford Anglia battles with a Lotus Ford Cortina at the British Saloon Car Championship at Brands Hatch, U.K., in 1965.*

▶▶ *Craig Lowndes leads the field during a typically closely fought race during the 2005 V8 Supercar Championship.*

TOURING CAR CHAMPIONSHIPS

From local and regional events for amateurs up to professional, international championships, there is an amazing array of different competitions for touring cars. Many countries—including Brazil, France, Japan, and Sweden—have national championships for touring cars that allow lesser or greater degrees of modification to the vehicles. The United States Touring Car Championship, for example, outlaws expensive racing suspension and transmissions, but it allows certain "bolt-on" parts to boost engine power up to around 200 horsepower. Some national championships, such as the British Touring Car Championship (BTCC), have expanded in order to attract foreign drivers and large crowds. The BTCC grew out of saloon car racing—a popular motorsport for amateur racers—and began back in 1958. For 2006, its schedule consisted of ten race weekends with three races per weekend, each one lasting around 20 laps. Such events put real pressure on teams to deliver a reliable yet competitive car for each race.

▶ *In round nine of the 2005 WTCC season at Valencia, Spain, British driver Andy Priaulx finished fourth in race one and third in race two on his way to winning the championship.*

► *Driving for Audi, Mattias Ekström took second place overall in the 2005 DTM. Here, he celebrates his victory at the Nürburgring in August 2005.*

Various international touring competitions have come and gone, including the original European Touring Car Championship (which ran in one form or another from 1963 to 1988 and again from 2001 to 2004) and the Touring Car World Cup (which ran from 1993 to 1995). Supported by the FIA, 2005 saw the launch of the World Touring Car Championship (WTCC). The first two seasons featured race weekends at ten famous circuits including Monza (Italy), Nevers Magny-Cours (France), and the Guia Circuit (Macau, China).

V8 SUPERCARS

The V8 Supercar Championship is a two-make series—an all-out battle between several teams (17 in 2005), all fielding either Ford or Holden vehicles. The competition developed out of national touring car championships in Australia, which have been held since 1960. V8 Supercars are monsters—the most highly powered of all touring cars—with a minimum weight of 2,981 lbs. (1,355kg) without the driver. The competition gets its name from the V8 engines that are supplied by Chevrolet (for the Holden cars) and Ford. These generate more than 600 horsepower and ensure high-speed racing, sometimes at speeds of more than 155mph (250km/h). The racing can be incredibly tight, often with only seconds separating the top ten finishers. Three races per weekend are common, and rounds of the championship include the famous Bathurst 1,000, as well as the Adelaide or Clipsal 500 (a street circuit) and races in New Zealand and Bahrain. At the start of 2006, a controversial new rule was introduced

at three race weekends. It sees the entire finishing order for the first race reversed so that the winner starts at the back of the grid for the second race, in which only half the points of the first race are available. At the start of 2006, the legendary Peter Brock still held the record of 37 V8 Supercar race wins. Mark Scaife was close with 36, but he still had a long way to go to match Brock's record of 100 podium finishes in Australian touring car championships.

▲ *Gary Paffett (Mercedes AMG) racing in round 11 of the 2005 DTM, at the Hockenheimring. The Briton won the championship after winning five races during the season.*

DEUTSCHE TOURENWAGEN MASTERS

Germany's Deutsche Tourenwagen Masters (DTM) is another prestigious competition that has an international following, but it is technically a national championship. Contested by factory teams and featuring heavily modified bodies and four-liter engines that generate up to 470 horsepower, the DTM began in 2000, replacing a similar competition that ran from 1984 to 1996. Each DTM race is around 99 miles (160km) long and stars an international cast of drivers. Eleven nationalities were represented in 2005: top drivers included Gary Paffett of the U.K., Sweden's Mattias Ekström (the 2004 winner), Le Mans legend Tom Kristensen of Denmark, three-time DTM champion Bernd Schneider of Germany, and former F1 world champion Mika Hakkinen of Finland. In 2006, the Audi works team featured DTM's female racer Vanina Ickx, daughter of the great Jacky Ickx. A major sporting event in its own country, DTM now extends beyond German borders: in 2004, it held an exhibition race in Shanghai, China; in 2005, there were races in the Czech Republic, Belgium, and Turkey; and in 2006, four of its ten races were held abroad (in the U.K., Spain, France, and the Netherlands).

►► *The American driver Mark Donohue races a Porsche 917/30 for Roger Penske in the 1973 Can-Am Series. He won this race at the Watkins Glen International track, New York State.*

PROTOTYPE AND GRAND TOURING

Sports car racing takes place on circuits and comes in many varieties. The two broad categories are prototype and grand touring (GT). Prototype vehicles are one-offs or limited editions that are built especially for racing. Since 1995, there have been two classes of prototypes that have been raced at Le Mans (see p. 38–39): the P1 monsters that weigh more than 2,000 lbs. (925kg) and have engines of up to six liters in size, and the slightly lighter and less powerful P2s. Grand touring vehicles have more in common with road cars, albeit expensive sports models from the likes of Lamborghini, Ferrari, Maserati, Porsche, and Aston Martin. Spectators enjoy grand touring because they get the chance to see beautiful sports cars in action. It is also the most popular group of classes of sports car racing. Grand touring competitions range from local events up to class racing at the Le Mans and Daytona 24 Hours. World Sportscar Championships ran under a range of names and

LE MANS SERIES

Following one year of the European Le Mans Series (ELMS) in 2000, the Le Mans Endurance Series (LMES) was launched in 2004 with races at historic circuits including Spa, Silverstone, and Nürburgring. Turkey's Istanbul Circuit was added in 2005; in 2006, the name was shortened to the Le Mans Series (LMS), and Silverstone was replaced by Donington. The races follow almost the same rules as the Le Mans 24 Hours, but they last 620 miles (1,000km), or six hours, and feature four classes, from GT production cars to the one-off LM (P1) beasts. The series winner and runner-up in each class gain automatic entry into the following year's Le Mans 24 Hours. More than 40 cars usually take part in each race, and the action is incredible: in the 2005 Silverstone 620 miles (1,000km), only 6.5 seconds separated first and second place.

▼ *Round four of the 2005 FIA GT Championship, raced in Imola, Italy. The cars of Enea Casoni, Edo Varini, and Marco Panzavuota lead the field.*

▼ *Paul Gentilozzi is chased by Klaus Graf during a 2005 Trans-Am race in Montreal, Canada. Gentilozzi withdrew after mechanical problems, and Graf, driving a Jaguar XKR, went on to win the championship.*

rules between 1953 and 1992. Since 1997, many top GT cars compete in the FIA GT Championship, which has races of at least 310 miles (500km) long that last up to three hours (one exception is the Spa 24 Hours). The racing is often exciting. For example, at the 2005 season opener in Monza, Italy, the top three cars were separated by less than 1.5 seconds and averaged more than 117mph (188km/h) over all 87 laps of the track. Most of the races are in Europe, but in 2006 one race was held in Dubai, United Arab Emirates. From 2007, the 998-mile (1,609-km) -long Mil Milhas Brasil (which translates as "the 1,000 miles of Brazil") will be part of the schedule too.

TRANS-AM AND CAN-AM

Two contrasting sports car racing series began in North America in 1966. The Trans-American Sedan Championship (Trans-Am Series) went on to become one of the longest-running road-racing series in North America. However, it entered 2006—its 40th year—facing an uncertain future, following the withdrawal of Champ Cars' support. The previous ten years were dominated by two drivers, Tommy Kendall and Paul Gentilozzi, who each claimed four championships and came in equal at first on points in 2004. The Canadian-American Challenge Cup (Can-Am), which ran until 1974, was one of the most unrestricted classes ever, with no limits on aerodynamic features or engine size. The resulting vehicles were monsters, topping 229mph (370km/h) on long straights and sporting cutting-edge innovations—such as wings and fans to create downforce. Can-Am attracted many of the top drivers of the day, with New Zealander Denny Hulme its biggest star, winning 22 races.

AMERICAN ENDURANCE RACING

Two endurance race competitions began in 1999 in North America: the American Le Mans Series (ALMS) and Grand-Am events. The latter comprise four series, one of which is the Rolex Sports Car Series that features the prestigious Daytona 24 Hours race, which has run since 1966. The ALMS features racing in both prototype and grand touring classes. The 2005 and 2006 seasons

both had ten races. Most are "sprints" lasting around two hours and 45 minutes, but the calendar also includes the ten-hour or 998-mile (1,609-km) -long Petit Le Mans race and the 12 Hours of Sebring, which has run since 1952 and is the oldest dedicated sports car race in the United States. Sebring winners have included Bobby Rahal, Juan Manuel Fangio, Mario Andretti, and Tom Kristensen. Porsche 911s, 934s, 935s, and 962s won 13 straight victories in the 1970s and 1980s, while the Audi R8 car won each year from 2000 to 2005. Points are awarded in each class after every ALMS race, and the team with the most points in each class at the season's end is invited to the following year's Le Mans 24 Hours.

▲ France's Sébastien Dumez drives his Chrysler Viper GTS-R in a French GT Championship race in Pau, France, in June 2003.

▼ 2004 ALMS champion J. J. Lehto races his Audi R8 during the Petit Le Mans race at Road Atlanta, Georgia. Audi R8s dominated the series in the early 2000s.

LE MANS 24 HOURS

There are a number of legendary endurance races around the world, but none is more famous or prestigious than the Le Mans 24 Hours. Since its founding in 1923 by the Automobile Club de l'Ouest (AOC), Le Mans has provided an amazing spectacle—one that attracts more than 350,000 spectators every June.

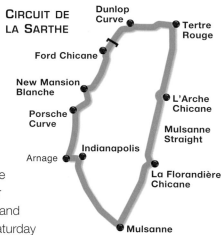

CIRCUIT DE LA SARTHE

Dunlop Curve
Tertre Rouge
Ford Chicane
New Mansion Blanche
L'Arche Chicane
Porsche Curve
Mulsanne Straight
Arnage
Indianapolis
La Florandière Chicane
Mulsanne

THE CIRCUIT

Le Mans' Circuit de la Sarthe consists of roads that are normally used by the public, as well as sections that were built for the race, including the 2.59-mile (4.18-km) -long Bugatti Circuit, which hosts touring car races and other events. Originally 10.7 miles (17.26km) long, the circuit has seen many changes, but since 1931, it has measured eight to nine miles (13–14km) long. Its famous features include the semicircular Dunlop Bridge and the 2.9-mile (4.6-km) -long Mulsanne Straight. Despite adding chicanes, this is still the fastest section of track, with speeds soaring to above 186mph (300km/h) before drivers have to brake hard for the tight and slippery Mulsanne corner at under 62mph (100km/h).

▲ The famous Le Mans start, where drivers ran across the track to their cars before starting, lasted from 1925 to 1969.

THE CHALLENGE

Around 50 cars take on the challenge of racing at high speeds for hour after hour. After days of scrutiny, practice, and qualifying, the race itself begins on Saturday afternoon. For the two or three drivers racing each vehicle, it is an incredible test of concentration, stamina, and driving techniques. The aim is to cover the greatest distance around the circuit in 24 hours of continuous racing. Drivers have to contend with changing weather conditions, mist and fog, and cars in different classes that may be up to 62mph (100km/h) slower or faster or that handle in a different way to their own. They complete tens of thousands of gear changes, knowing that a single gear change error at such a high speed can destroy an engine. In between racing stints, drivers try to rest, but many find this impossible due to the adrenaline rush of the race. Fatigue in later sessions of the race can prove costly, however—just one missed racing line on the 350-plus laps that they cover during the race may see the car crash out. In the pits, teams have to be ready for anything, from complete brake changes to patching up bodywork or replacing a

▼ France's Henri Pescarolo is a Le Mans legend, having won the 24 Hour race on four occasions and started it a record of 33 times.

▼ Great Britain's Johnny Herbert races his Audi R8 in 2004. The car finished second behind the Audi of six-time winner Tom Kristensen, Seiji Ara, and Rinaldo Capello.

www.teamveloqx.c

veloqx visionz inc.

transmission. Many cars do not finish—in 1970, only seven out of 51 vehicles completed the race. Regular pit stops are essential for fuel, tire, and driver changes, as well as any running repairs that are required. But even with more than 20 stops, winning cars average an incredible speed of more than 124mph (200km/h). Despite the huge challenges that the race poses for drivers, teams, and machinery, Le Mans has an allure that sees teams and drivers coming back again and again.

RECORD BREAKERS

Held more than 70 times in the past 83 years, the Le Mans 24 Hours has seen numerous outstanding races, with many records made and broken. In 1923, the first winning car traveled 1,370 miles (2,209km). Eight years later, an Alfa Romeo was the first to complete 1,860 miles (3,000km) in the 24 hours of racing. The distance records kept increasing, with the record for the greatest distance covered being set in 1971. Gijs van Lennep and Helmut Marko's Porsche 917 raced a staggering 3,308mph (5,335km)—an average speed of 137.8mph (222.2km/h). Speed-limiting changes to the course have ensured that the record still stands.

There are prizes for different classes of vehicles, but the ultimate aim is an overall win. An overall victory has usually guaranteed a boost in sales for the winning manufacturer, from Bentley's four

wins in a row from 1927, through Jaguar's five wins in the 1950s, Ferrari's six in the 1960s, and Porsche's seven consecutive titles in the 1980s. Porsche remains the leading winner, with 16 overall Le Mans victories by 2006. The record-winning margin was set in 1927 when a Bentley Sport car finished 216.9 miles (349.8km) ahead of second place, but there have been some very close finishes. In 1969, Jacky Ickx and Jackie Oliver raced their Ford GT40 a distance of 3,099 miles (4,998km) to win, yet the second-placed Porsche was only 394 feet (120m) behind. Three years earlier, two Ford GT40s crossed the line together in a staged finish. Officials ruled that, as Le Mans is a distance race, the car that started lower down the grid had traveled farther and therefore won.

▲ The S101 Judd car of the Dutch team Holland Dome competes in the 2005 Le Mans 24 Hours.

▼ Woolf Barnato, pictured in his Bentley Speed Six, won the Le Mans 24 Hours three times in a row, from 1928 to 1930.

RALLYING, RALLYCROSS, AND OFF-ROAD

Rally racing is one of the most popular of all motorsports—thousands of amateurs take part in club rallying on roads and courses. At the other end of the scale, extremely talented racers enter major competitions such as the World Rally Championship (WRC), which is considered to be one of the ultimate tests of any driver's skills.

A CLASS APART

Rallying stands apart from many other forms of racing. It involves two racers per car (a driver and a codriver), takes place across a wide and challenging variety of terrains, and can last a number of days. Instead of all cars starting at the same time, most rallies see individual cars start a section, known as a special stage, of a rally alone. Cars race from point to point against the clock, aiming for all of their times at the special stages to add up to less than their rivals' times, taking into account any time penalties that have been incurred. Rallying attracts surprisingly little media attention, given its status in many countries as the leading class of motorsports. National championships and WRC rallies draw staggeringly large crowds—as many as one million live spectators for a single WRC rally.

THE WORLD RALLY CHAMPIONSHIP

The pinnacle of rallying is the World Rally Championship, run under FIA rules, which began in 1973. Around 16 incredibly challenging rallies are held each season, with points running 10-8-6-5-4-3-2-1 for the top eight finishers. These points count toward the drivers' championship, while the

combined points total of two team cars goes toward the manufacturers' championship. Each rally usually consists of 14 to 27 special stages, with driving on normal roads between each stage (a typical day's driving amounts to around 248 miles, or 400km). WRC rallies run according to a strict timetable, with penalties for late or early arrival at a stage or in or out of the service parks—usually ten seconds per minute late. Each WRC rally is usually 744 to 1,116 miles (1,200–1,800km) long; the Tour de Corse, the Rally of France held in Corsica, is a little shorter, at around 620 miles (1,000km), but it takes place on roads that twist and wind alongside hair-raising drops of up to 984 feet (300m). Each rally poses a different challenge. Slippery forest tracks characterize the Rally of Australia and the Wales Rally GB; asphalt and dust are part of the challenge at the Rally of Japan; the Rally of Sweden is raced on snow, gravel, and, sometimes, ice. The Rally of Argentina is renowned for its many rivers, which drivers must cross with skill and speed; the Cyprus Rally is the slowest WRC event with its twisting, rock-strewn roads. The Acropolis Rally in Greece and the Rally of Turkey are both feared for their unforgiving, razor-sharp gravel. In the Rally of Finland, cars have to contend with very bumpy ground—which means many jumps. To win the WRC, a driver needs smart teamwork, a superb codriver, lightning reactions, and consummate driving skills in all conditions.

▲ Scotland's Colin McRae competes in the 2001 Acropolis Rally in a Ford Focus WRC. After four days of hard racing, he won the rally by just 49 seconds.

▼ Sebastian Loeb in his Citroën Xsara WRC races against Petter Solberg's Subaru Impreza during the super special stage of the 2005 Acropolis Rally at Athens' Olympic stadium.

◄◄ Driving for Team Red Devil Atolye Kazaz, Finland's Kristian Sohlberg, and Kaj Lindstrom compete in the 2006 Rally of Sweden. They retired after their Subaru Impreza had engine trouble.

OTHER MAJOR CHAMPIONSHIPS

Many countries hold their own national rallying championships, and the FIA endorses four regional competitions: the Asia-Pacific, Middle East, African, and European Rally Championships. The United States Rally Championship began in 2005 with four events; its 2006 season featured eight, six of which were recognized by the FIA, and therefore able to accept international entries. Running alongside the WRC are the FIA Production Car World Rally and the Junior World Rally Championship (JWRC). The latter began in 2001 and is for drivers under 28 years of age who race cars with only two-wheel drive and power restrictions. The JWRC features fewer events than

the WRC—only nine events in 2006—but the rallies themselves are still extremely challenging. In its short history, the JWRC has been an excellent proving ground for younger drivers. Its first champion was French rally driver Sebastian Loeb, who went on to win the World Rally Championship in 2004 and 2005. The JWRC also gives a chance for teams to build up experience relatively cheaply. Suzuki, whose driver Per-Gunnar Andersson won the 2004 JWRC crown, now plans to enter a team in the WRC from August 2007.

◀ During the 2001 Tour de Corse, Tommi Mäkinen (in red) paces beside his wrecked car, which is perched precariously on the lip of a sheer drop.

▲ The 2005 FIA Middle East Rally Championship was made up of nine rallies, including the three-day Jordan Rally shown here.

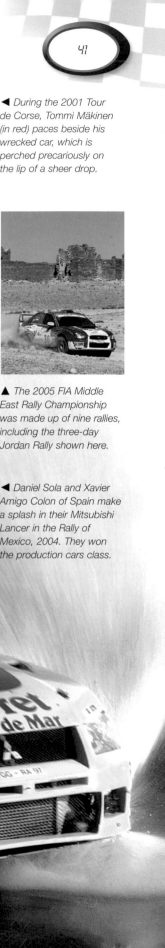

◀ Daniel Sola and Xavier Amigo Colon of Spain make a splash in their Mitsubishi Lancer in the Rally of Mexico, 2004. They won the production cars class.

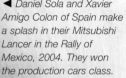

ONE TOUGH CAR

Part of rally driving's spectator appeal is the fact that the cars look like the hatchbacks and saloon cars that the public drive themselves. The rules state that the cars must be based on a four-seater production model of which at least 25,000 have been built. Look closer, though, and you will see that top rally cars are heavily modified, high-performance monsters that generate more than three times the horsepower of their production cousins and cost around $750,000 to build. They contain two seats with racing harnesses and a tough internal roll cage made out of strong safety tubing. Rally cars need astonishing stopping power, and this is provided by huge, carbon-fiber brake rotors. The front disks on the 2003 championship-winning Citroën Xsara T4 WRC, for example, measured 15 inches (37.6cm) in diameter, bigger than many road cars' actual wheels. These can glow red-hot after heavy use. Rally cars' tires are also wider than road vehicles': around nine inches (225mm) for use on asphalt roads, a little narrower for gravel, and much narrower (5–6 inches, or 135–145mm), with metal studs, for snow and ice.

▲ A selection of Michelin tires used in round one of the 2003 World Rally Championship—the famous Monte Carlo Rally.

▲ Estonian driver Markko Märtin tests his car in France in December 2003. World rally cars have a range of safety features, including a welded-in roll cage to protect the driver and codriver.

LIFE IN THE SERVICE PARK

A WRC rally is one of racing's most severe tests of a car's power, handling, toughness, and reliability. Teams are allowed to perform some running repairs, but only at set times and under strict scrutiny. Teams only get to work on their cars for 30 minutes after a group of stages and are also given a longer 45-minute session at the end of each day before the car is locked up in the *parc fermé*. Rally cars take a pounding through the special stages, and the team may have a battle against the clock to get all of its repairs done without incurring penalties. Cars often radio ahead before completing the stage to warn their team of any major damage. Service park teams

▲ Subaru mechanics work as fast as they can to service Norwegian Petter Solberg's car at the service park in Swansea during the 2005 Wales Rally GB.

▶ Spectacular jumps take their toll on a rally car's suspension. Here, Petter Solberg's Subaru Impreza WRC takes off during the 2004 Rally of Finland.

of ten or more technicians have to contend with everything from battered side panels to worn brakes and damaged suspension.

DRIVER AND CODRIVER

WRC rallies and many others allow cars to perform a complete reconnaissance, or recce, of the stages beforehand. The codriver compiles crucial "pacenotes"—accurate and incredibly comprehensive details of each stage's features, including every potential obstacle, every change in surface, and every bend, the severity of which is usually graded from one to five. Using these pacenotes and an intercom system inside of the car, the codriver guides the driver precisely through each special stage. A driver must trust the codriver completely, as he or she is directed around a blind corner or along a narrow track obscured by mist, rain, or twilight. The driver must also be ready for anything as the car rounds a bend or launches over a rise, all at terrifyingly high speeds and with little margin for error. Aside from possessing extraordinarily quick reactions, rally drivers need a range of specific skills, including the ability to time jumps, to power through river crossings, and to apply opposite lock (see p. 65) to slide sideways around gravel-surfaced corners.

RALLYCROSS

Originating in Europe in the late 1960s, rallycross is a mixture of rallying and circuit racing. It takes place over a small number of laps of a course that mix asphalt track, gravel, and dirt, with cars all starting at the same time. The biggest championship is the European Rallycross Championship (ERC), where the action is fast and furious. The ERC has a series of qualifying races in which cars start five across; a lot of bumping and buffeting follow as they fight for position. Qualifying races determine grid positions in the C, B, and A finals. These races each involve six cars, starting in three rows of two, all intent on getting to the first corner in the lead. There are divisions within rallycross, with Division One featuring the most powerful cars. Scandinavia dominates rallycross, and Sweden's Kenneth Hansen is the star of Division One, having won the ERC championship for six years in a row (2000–2005).

OFF-ROAD AND RALLY RAIDS

Off-road racing, as its name indicates, takes place away from roads—often through incredibly harsh terrains such as deserts, icy or rocky plateaus, and hills. Off-road racing is popular in Australia and especially in the U.S., where there are numerous off-road associations. These include Best in the Desert (BITD), which puts on several series of races; Championship Off-Road Racing (CORR), which held a nine-race season in 2006;

and Score International, which organizes numerous events, including the famous Baja 1,000. Cross-country rallies and long-distance rally raids, such as the UAE Desert Challenge and the world-famous Dakar Rally, are popular. Other tough events include the Por Las Pampas Rally, with a route stretching more than 3,000 miles (4,800km) along South America's west coast, and northern India's 1,550-mile (2,500-km) -long Raid de Himalaya, which crosses some of the world's highest mountain passes.

▲ At the 2006 Rally of Mexico, Spanish driver Daniel Sordo powers his Citroën Xsara through the Mexican state of Leon, on the way to fourth place overall.

◄ Gaurav Chiripal crosses a bridge in his Maruti Gypsy during the 2003 Raid de Himalaya. The four-day rally passes through the northern Indian mountain valleys of Lahul, Spiti, and Ladakh.

MOTORCYCLE RACING

Motorcycle racing has as rich of a pedigree as racing on four wheels. Today, there is a huge range of events, but each one of them requires fantastic balance, great courage, and excellent riding skills.

▲ *Valentino Rossi has dominated MotoGP in recent years. However, several up-and-coming riders are now seeking to claim the Italian's crown.*

► *Australian rider Anthony West wheelies toward the finish line to win the Dutch 250cc GP at the Assen Circuit in June 2003.*

▼ *Italian MotoGP rider Loris Capirossi is thrown off his Ducati in a crash at the 2004 Japanese GP. Fortunately, he was not seriously injured.*

FROM TT TO MOTOGP

Early motorcycles and tricycles contested some of the first city-to-city races in Europe at the start of the 1900s. The Isle of Man Tourist Trophy (see p. 78) admitted motorcycles for the first time in 1907 and quickly became Europe's premier motorcycle race. While dirt-track racing, speedway, and motocross all developed in the years between the two World Wars, Grand Prix racing on circuits began in the U.S. and Europe. The FIM Road Racing World Championship Grand Prix series, now known as MotoGP, began in 1949. Starting with four classes based on bikes with 125cc, 250cc, 350cc, and 500cc engines, it quickly became the pinnacle of motorcycle-circuit racing. Over time, these classes changed. For example, the 350cc class was dropped in 1982, while a 50cc class ran from 1962 to 1983, and an 80cc class ran from 1984 to 1989. In 2002, the MotoGP class replaced the top-level 500cc machines, with bikes of up to 990cc permitted (this was reduced to 800cc from 2007). No expense is spared on these high-powered machines, which use advanced materials, such as carbon fiber and titanium, and incorporate traction control and other examples of cutting-edge technology. MotoGP bikes develop up to 230 horsepower and can reach speeds of more than 210mph (340km/h). Yet the amount of the tire that is in contact with the ground is little more than the size of a human hand, requiring riders to demonstrate amazing control and balance as they rocket around a circuit. MotoGP races vary in length depending on the track, but most of them tend to last a distance of 68–74 miles (110–120km), comprise

20 to 30 laps, and take around 45 minutes to complete. MotoGP races are held worldwide in countries such as China, Malaysia, and Australia, as well as in traditional European strongholds such as Italy, Germany, and Great Britain. As MotoGP is the pinnacle of motorcycle road racing, large crowds are always guaranteed to watch the world's best riders in action—these include the Spaniards Sete Gibernau and Daniel Pedrosa, Italians Valentino Rossi and Loris Capirossi, and Americans Nicky Hayden and Colin Edwards.

SUPERBIKES

Superbikes are production motorcycles that have been modified according to strict rules for racing on tracks. Teams can alter only a few specific features of the bikes, which are monsters with engines between 900 and 1,000cc in size. Although they are only marginally slower, Superbikes are much cheaper to buy and run than MotoGP machines. They still develop 210 horsepower— around double that of a family saloon car— and can race along tracks at speeds of up to 198mph (320km/h). Several countries have

▲ MotoGP rider Nicky Hayden of the U.S. speeds through a bend on his Honda during the 2005 Australian GP.

national Superbike championships, including Japan, Australia, and Great Britain. One of the first, and, arguably, biggest, national competitions is the American Motorcycling Association (AMA) Superbike Championship. Started in 1976, it now draws huge crowds and media interest as it tours 11 U.S. circuits, including Laguna Seca and Daytona, alongside other motorcycle classes such as Superstock and Supersport. The sport's most dominant rider in recent times has been Australia's Mat Mladin, who won the championship on six occasions between 1999 and 2005.

WORLD SUPERBIKES

Beginning in 1988, the World Superbike Championship (WSBK) is a major track-racing competition that is mostly run on European circuits—although the 2006 series began in Qatar, moved on to Australia, and finished in South Africa. The races are run over a distance of around 62 miles (100km), with the number of laps varying according to the length of the circuit. There are usually two races per weekend, with the 2006 series featuring 13 rounds and 26 races. Some riders, like talented Australian Chris Vermeulen, use the competition as a stepping-stone to MotoGP. Others stick with it such as Noriyuki Haga, 1996 champion Troy Corser of Australia (who was also the first nonAmerican to win the AMA Superbikes title since 1978), and the dominant rider of the 1990s, Carl Fogarty, who won 59 races and four WSBK crowns.

▲ Flames spit out from the exhaust of the Kawasaki ridden by Fonsi Nieto during the Australian round of the 2006 World Superbike Championship.

◄◄ Tommy Hayden (1) and Jason Disalvo (40) battle for position during an AMA Superstock race at the Infineon Raceway in Sonoma, California, in May 2005.

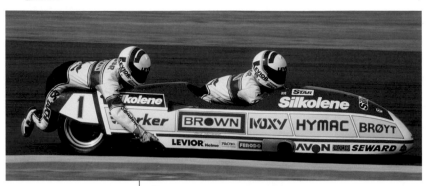

▲ *The passenger in sidecar racing must leap around the vehicle and lean at dramatic angles in order to maintain balance. Here, Tony Hewitt (left) and Steve Webster race in 1989, the year in which they won a third world title in a row.*

▲ *Belgian motocross star Stefan Everts shows great control as he jumps high up into the air. By the end of 2005, Everts had won a remarkable nine world titles and 87 Grand Prix.*

▶▶ *Jeremy McGrath takes a bend during a practice for the opening round of the 2006 AMA Supercross Championship, held at Anaheim, California.*

ON THREE WHEELS

Motorcycle sidecar racing was a feature of the very first GP World Championship in 1949 and was part of that competition until 1997, when it moved onto the World Superbike calendar. Now known as the Superside Sidecar World Championship, 2005 saw it embark on a Europe-wide series of rounds held in Croatia, Germany, Sweden, and the Netherlands, among other nations. Vintage sidecars consisted of a separate unit that was bolted onto the motorcycle's side, but modern racing sidecars are all-in-one machines with a monocoque design. Racing is an exciting spectacle, with the sidecar passenger throwing himself or herself around and leaning at extreme angles to help the rider and their vehicle corner at high speeds. The vehicles can accelerate from 0–60mph (0–100km/h) in around three seconds, and at Monza in 2001, ten-time world champion Steve Webster was clocked at 174mph (281km/h) at one point. Motorcycle sidecars are also raced in other classes, including trials, vintage rallies, and sidecar-cross— a form of motocross. Swiss company LCR is the leading sidecar racing constructor. It won 21 world titles between 1980 and the end of 2005.

MOTOCROSS AND SUPERCROSS

It is estimated that more people take part in motocross than in any other form of motorcycle racing. Motocross riders race over a closed off-road circuit that uses the natural features of the terrain such as jumps, hills, ditches, and ruts. As many as 40 riders start in a motocross event. They race over a set number of laps of the circuit,

which makes huge demands on riders' strength and stamina as they slide around corners, bounce heavily over bumps called whoops, and make jumps as high as 20 feet (6m). Motocross bikes feature chunky tread tires and very large shock absorbers to cushion the impact of the heavy landings. Long "banana'"seats allow the rider to shift their body weight forward or backward in order to keep the vehicle under control.

Supercross is an arena-based version of motocross, featuring shorter artificial courses. It demands excellent control as the racers contend with tight tracks with many twists and turns, multiple bumps, triple jumps, and table-top plateaus with steep slopes on both sides. It has become the most popular motorcycling sport in the U.S. and is frequently televised. The AMA 250cc Supercross Championship and the AMA East and West 125cc titles are the sport's most prestigious competitions in the U.S., with riders such as Ricky Carmichael, Jeremy McGrath, and James "Bubba" Stewart its major stars.

Arenacross is an even more scaled-down version of motocross that can be held in indoor arenas, while supermoto is similar to rallycross for cars and features bikes that race on a circuit that mostly consist of track, but with some off-road features, including jumps.

DIRT TRACKERS

Dirt-track racing has been popular on short courses, especially in North America, for many decades. Speedway is a form of dirt-track racing that is especially well supported in Scandinavia, Great Britain, Eastern Europe, and Oceania. Speedway's 500cc motorbikes are powered by methanol and

▲ Sweden's Tony Rickardsson is a legend in speedway. He claimed his sixth world title in 2005.

▼ Riders scramble over dunes during the 2001 Enduro du Touquet race. First held in 1975, this 10.4-mile (16.8-km) -long endurance race attracts more than 900 riders and 250,000 spectators.

have no gears or brakes—a stunning fact when you see riders flash around a short oval track, sliding their vehicles through the turns at alarming angles and speeds. The racing is fast and furious, with four riders competing in a series of four-lap races that each last around one minute. Teams and individual riders compete in national leagues, and the British, Polish, Swedish, and Danish leagues are especially good. National teams enter the Speedway World Cup, while top individuals compete in the Speedway GP circuit, which has ten events in Latvia, Poland, and the Czech Republic, among other countries.

OFF-ROAD ACTION

Trials are competitions that are run on obstacle-laden courses over natural rocky terrain or artificial courses inside of arenas. Speed is less important than balance, concentration, and precision bike handling as riders aim to complete the course without their feet or body touching the ground or leaning against an obstacle. Competitors use specialist lightweight bikes that weigh as little as 154 lbs. (70kg) and have a low center of gravity to give the rider as much stability as possible. Trials courses tend to be over short distances. At the other end of the spectrum are long-distance off-road events and rally raids that include classes for motorcycles such as the Baja 1,000 and the Dakar Rally. Enduro is a form of on- and off-road racing with some similarities to car rallying, in which riders complete in measured stages and reach checkpoints within the allowed time. The International Six Days Enduro, first held in 1913, tests riders and machines over six days and 1,240 miles (2,000km) of grueling racing.

OTHER CLASSES

There are dozens of motorsport classes and competitions that, while not as well known as the likes of NASCAR and F1, still attract thousands of racers and fans. Below, we take a look at some of these varied forms of racing.

MIDGETS, LEGENDS, AND SPRINTS

Scaled-down cars racing on short tracks are very popular in North America. Legends racing, for example, features scaled-down replicas of classic American cars from the 1930s and 1940s. These 5/8th-scale vehicles, all built by 600 Racing, Inc., and costing less than $20,000, are starting to also be raced in the U.K. and Europe. Midget cars boomed in popularity in the years before and after World War II, but they are still raced today, usually on short tracks over distances of less than 25 miles (40km) per race. Sprint cars are a little larger, more powerful, and faster than midget cars and mostly race on dirt or clay ovals at speeds sometimes in excess of 124mph (200km/h). Their bodies are amazingly simple: they have a tubular frame and roll cage, a power-packed engine, and a large fuel tank that is filled with methanol. The Sprint Car Racing Association (SCRA) runs the best-known series for sprint cars without wings. Other competitions, such as the famous World of Outlaws Championship, feature cars with aerodynamic wings that are mounted on the top of their roll cages in order to generate downforce and keep the cars on the ground.

RACE OF CHAMPIONS

Since 1988, the Race of Champions (ROC) has provided end-of-season glamour as some of motorsports' best rally- and circuit-racing drivers set their wits and skills against each other. The most recent editions have been staged on a twisting course at the Stade de France stadium in Paris, France. Pairs of drivers compete head-to-head in identical vehicles, which vary through the rounds and include a Citroën Xsara WRC car and an ROC buggy, designed by Honda. Heats lead to finals for the rally and circuit-racing stars; the winner of each final enters the Superfinal. In 1999, an ROC Nations Cup was added to the competition, usually with eight countries taking part. The event has tended to favor rally drivers— Sebastien Loeb was the individual champion in 2005, but others have triumphed recently. The 2004 winner, Heikki Kovalainen, raced in GP2 in 2005 and the following year was an F1 test driver for Renault, while the 2002 Nations Cup-winning U.S. team included Jeff Gordon and Jimmie Johnson from NASCAR.

▲ *Heikki Kovalainen (right) of Finland edges his Renault Mégane ahead of Denmark's Tom Kristensen at the 2005 Race of Champions.*

▼ *Formula One ace Michael Schumacher gets airborne in a racing buggy during the Race of Champions in 2004.*

▲ *Steve Kinser (driving the green car) is a legend in sprint racing. Between 1978 and 2005, he won an extraordinary 20 World of Outlaws Championships.*

◄ *Midget racing action at the 2002 American GP at Indianapolis, Indiana.*

DRAG RACING

The ultimate in acceleration action, drag racing involves short bursts of amazingly fast racing. Races usually take place between two vehicles from a standing start along a straight drag strip over a distance of either 1,319 feet (402m, or one quarter of a mile) or 659 feet (201m, or one eighth of a mile). Since the 1950s, the National Hot Rod Association (NHRA) has organized the biggest and best drag races in the U.S. The two main classes of drag racing are Top Fuel and Funny Cars. Top Fuel cars run on racing alcohol—an explosive mixture that generates around 3.4 times as much power as gasoline. These cars can accelerate at astonishing speeds—from 0–100mph (0–160km/h) in just 0.8 seconds. In contrast to the long, thin bodies of Top Fuel dragsters, Funny Cars are heavier, chunkier vehicles with engines of around eight liters that are mounted in front of the driver and a body that is jacked up at the back to allow room for giant rear wheels. These accelerate just a fraction slower than

Top Fuel dragsters, but they can attain similar (and sometimes faster) top speeds. Racing is head-to-head over a series of rounds, with the loser eliminated after each race. The Christmas tree—the arrangement of starting lights—signals the start of the race. Light sensors measure the elapsed time (the time it takes to complete the race) and the top speed, which is measured in a speed trap during the last 66 feet (20m) of the race. The speeds that are attained by the fastest drag racers are amazing. On the way to winning the 2005 NHRA Top Fuel Championship, Tony Schumacher covered the 659-foot (201-m) -long course in just 4.437 seconds and hit a top speed of just over 335mph (540km/h).

▲ *Thomas Nataas accelerates hard in his "Batmobil" Funny Car during the European Drag Racing finals at the Santa Pod Raceway, U.K., in 2003.*

▼ *Tony Schumacher launches his Top Fuel drag racer down the track at Infineon Raceway, California, in 2005.*

HILL CLIMBING

Hill climbing has a long history—the U.K.'s Shelsley Walsh Hill Climb, which was first run in 1905, is the world's oldest surviving motorsports competition to still be staged at the same course. Drivers race against the clock, often after taking a trial run in which they try to post the fastest time along an uphill course. These can be short, sharp, sub-one-minute sprints up steep inclines or longer, winding courses with many tight bends. The Pikes Peak International Hill Climb (see p. 79) is almost 12.4 miles (20km) long, while New Zealand's famous Race to the Sky is 9.3 miles (15km) long and features more than 130 corners. Different types of vehicles race in hill climb competitions in their own classes, including motorcycle sidecars, quad bikes, and even racing trucks. The fastest entrants tend to be modified rally or off-road cars or specialist single-seater hill climbers.

FORMULA WOMAN AND GP MASTERS

The Formula Woman Championship began in the U.K. in 2004, solely for female drivers. In 2006, it became the Nations Cup—an international competition in which Caterham Roadsport B cars are raced over an eight-round championship. GP Masters has taken its lead from veterans' competitions in other sports such as golf and tennis. It pits some of the most famous ex-Formula One drivers over the age of 45 against each other. Racers in the inaugural event included Nigel Mansell, René Arnoux, Alain Prost, and Emerson Fittipaldi—the oldest of the 14 drivers, who turned 60 in December 2006. After a single successful race at Kyalami in South Africa in 2005, the following year saw races held at Monza in Italy and Silverstone

▲ Female drivers compete in the first-ever Formula Woman Championship in 2004.

in the U.K., among other circuits. With drivers racing Delta Motorsport cars generating a fearsome 600 horsepower and providing top speeds of more than 192mph (310km/h), this was no gentle procession, but a chance for fans to see drivers renew old friendships and rivalries and test themselves, once again, behind the wheel.

KARTS AND SUPERKARTS

The world of karting has provided an affordable starting point for several of motor racing's greatest stars. The sport's huge popularity is shown by the wide range of kart racing in existence, from casual or beginners' racing in karts without transmissions to high-performance models with five- or six-speed transmissions and a top speed of more than 93mph (150km/h). Most karts do not have suspension and instead rely on some give in their chassis to absorb small bumps in the track. Kart racing is usually held on short tracks and are either endurance contests or, more commonly, sprints that last up to 15 minutes per race. At the top end, karting requires great skill, and events such as the World Superkart Association's series or the CIK-FIA's World Karting Championship are incredibly competitive.

Superkarts are a step up in power and speed. The top-class Division One karts are powered by 250cc engines, are capable of 0–60mph (0–100km/h) in around three seconds, and have a top speed of around 149mph (240km/h). Due to their amazing cornering and braking abilities (they can slow down to a halt from 99mph, or 160km/h, in two seconds), these vehicles are serious racers; at some circuits, superkarts can outpace top sports cars. Many competitions race on long circuits of around one mile (1.5km) in length. The 2005 European Superkart Championship, for example, featured racing on famous motorsports tracks, including Hockenheim and Assen.

▲ Former F1 drivers wave to the crowds at the GP Masters event in South Africa in November 2005. The race was won by 1992 F1 champion Nigel Mansell.

◄◄ Fellow competitors cheer on Clint Vahsholtz in his Ford Mustang as he wins the Super Stock category of the 2003 Pikes Peak International Hill Climb in Colorado.

▶ Up-and-coming kart driver Kazeem Manzur races at Parma's Kartdromo, Italy, in March 2006.

ROLLING BACK THE YEARS

Part of motor racing's appeal is its heritage and its thousands of beautiful, and sometimes fragile, vehicles of the past. Many of these vehicles are paraded in gentle rallies or raced surprisingly hard in intense competitions, where technical advances, especially in tire technology and engine tuning, can see them post even faster times than when they were in their prime. There are hundreds of different events for vintage vehicles, from circuit racing to historic hill climbs, and all sorts of vehicles are raced, from popular classic production cars such as Minis, Ford Cortinas, and MGs, to exotic Can-Am and old Formula One machines. The FIA runs a number of championships for historic cars, including historic hill climb and rally events, as well as the popular GTC '65 competition for Grand Touring sports cars made before 1966. In the U.K.,

standout events include the Goodwood Revival and the Goodwood Festival of Speed, while in the US., the famous Laguna Seca Circuit hosts the Rolex Monterey Historic Automobile races, which, in their 32nd year in 2005, attracted more than 400 vintage race vehicles.

▲ *Vintage vehicles compete for the 2005 Brooklands Trophy at the Goodwood Revival event in Goodwood, U.K.*

▲ *Superkart racing is incredibly fast-paced and competitive. Some events attract racers from F1 and other premier motorsports. Here, Indy Racing League's Tony Kanaan leads the 12-hour Granja Viana race in Brazil, in November 2004.*

WACKY RACES

If it moves, race it! That is the motto of some ingenious and thrill-seeking racers as they propel a surprising array of vehicles, from lawn mowers to school buses, around tracks, over obstacles, and on ice.

"GRASSROOTS" RACING

Rider mowers, with their cutting blades removed, have been adapted and used for low-speed racing ever since a group of British motorsports enthusiasts, bemoaning the cost of entering motor racing, came up with the idea in 1973. The British Lawn Mower Racing Association divides motorized lawn mowers into three groups. Group Two consists of lawn mowers with a grass-collecting hopper on the front. Group Three vehicles are more like go-karts, with no hood, while Group Four features garden tractors with more powerful engines. A similar U.S. organization was formed in 1992, with 20 different state organizations and a major sponsor. One of the most famous and longest-running lawn mower races is the U.K.'s 12 Hours of Wisborough Green—an endurance

▲ Fans watch a school bus race at the Rocky Mountain National Speedway, Colorado, in July 2005.

race for lawn mowers that pays homage to the great Le Mans 24 Hours race. Run overnight, and with driver changes and refueling, the top lawn mowers can cover more than 298 miles (480km) in the race. A former member of a winning team at this event was none other than the legendary Stirling Moss!

MONSTERS AND MIDGETS

When it comes to racing big vehicles, trucks, supertrucks, and monster trucks are about as big as it gets. Monster trucks are oversize four-wheel-drive vehicles with tires that are 5.2 feet (1.6m) high or larger and giant suspension systems that allow them to clamber over cars and other large obstacles. Hundreds of events are held all over the world, but the true home of the sport is the U.S., where most races—usually in the form of two trucks competing head-to-head over two identical obstacle courses—are run by the United States Hot Rod Association.

The racing of powerful truck cabs, which are normally used to haul large trailers of cargo, developed in the U.S. in the early 1980s, and there are now national competitons in countries including France, the U.K., and Brazil. Since the mid 1980s, the European Truck Racing Cup has featured a series of races held at famous circuits, including Zolder in Belgium, Catalunya in Spain, and Nogaro in France. With a speed limit of 99mph (160km/h), this competition sees some incredibly tight racing, as trucks weighing a minimum of 12,100 lbs. (5,500kg—more than three times the weight of a NASCAR Craftsman Truck) speed around the track. And power is truly the word—Red Line Racing's Volvo FH truck, for example, can accelerate from 0–60mph (0–100km/h) quicker than a Ferrari 355 sports car.

At the other end of the spectrum are tiny, scaled-down motorcycles known as pocket bikes. At around one quarter of the size of a regular motorcycle, pocket bikes rarely have suspension systems, relying instead on their tires to absorb bumps on the track. Pocket bikes may look cute and are certainly an affordable and popular way for children to get into racing, but at the top end,

▲ A pocket bike rider corners in the rain at Kinsham Raceway in Powys, U.K., in 1996.

◄◄ A Group Two lawn mower in action at the 12 Hours of Wisborough Green endurance race.

they are taken very seriously by adult racers. Despite only generating a maximum of around 15 horsepower, the light weight of these vehicles means that the best models and riders can achieve speeds approaching 62mph (100km/h). The MotoGP ace Valentino Rossi, for example, was the Italian pocket bike champion twice.

ICE IS NICE

Racing on ice or heavily compacted snow using studded or spiked tires is popular in Canada, the U.S., Scandinavia, and Italy, but nowhere is it more popular than in France. The country has hosted a number of competitions for bikes and cars, including the famous 24 Hours of Chamonix race that attracted entrants such as Nigel Mansell, Ari Vatanen, and Stéphane Peterhansel until its cancellation in 2003. The Trophée Andros is a series of events around ice tracks, with a final race held in the Stade de France stadium. The 2005–2006 season featured former F1 champion Alain Prost among the entrants. At Extreme International Ice Racing (XiiR) events, spectators love the speeds on ice. Featuring a 20-plus race championship held in different parts of the U.S., speedway bikes and quad bikes, or ATVs, race on an indoor ice track, equipped with heavily studded tires but no brakes.

▲ Finnish ex-rally driver Markku Alen slides into trouble during a 1998 Trophée Andros ice race at Alpe d'Huez, France.

▲ A Mercedes-Benz Supertruck is put through its paces during a round of the European Truck Racing Cup, held at Thruxton, U.K., in June 1997.

◄ Monster truck "Grave Digger" smashes a vehicle during the Monster Truck Challenge at the Orange County Fair Speedway, New York, in 2004.

PHOTO FINISH
ALEX ZANARDI'S COMEBACK

Italy's Alessandro "Alex" Zanardi was a Formula One driver before switching to CART racing in 1996. He became one of the most popular racers in the competition and won the championship in 1997 and 1998 with Chip Ganassi Racing. In September 2001, Zanardi was leading a CART race at the Euro Speedway Circuit in Germany. Emerging from a pit stop, he lost control and was hit at high speed by Alex Tagliani's car. Quick medical help saved his life but could not save both of his legs from amputation. Zanardi refused to be beaten, however, and he began a courageous recovery with prosthetic legs. In 2003, he drove the 13 laps of the Euro Speedway Circuit that his accident had prevented him from completing. The following year, he entered the European Touring Car Championship in a specially equipped car, followed by the World Touring Car Championship. On August 28, 2005, Zanardi put the seal on his comeback by winning at Oschersleben in Germany. It was one of the most emotional wins in the history of motorsports, celebrated by both spectators and rival drivers.

▼ Alex Zanardi leads the field in a BMW 320i, on the way to his first victory in the World Touring Car Championship, at Germany's Oschersleben Circuit in 2005.

▲ Alex Zanardi gives a joyful victory salute after winning the touring car race at Oschersleben.

▼ Alex Tagliani's blue Ford-Reynard collides with Alex Zanardi's Honda-Reynard during the American Memorial 500 CART race in 2001.

A WINNING DESIGN

A modern racing vehicle is full of high-tech systems that are made out of the most advanced materials. An F1 car, for example, contains more than 5,000 parts, each one built to the highest specifications imaginable.

AERODYNAMICS AND DOWNFORCE

Aerodynamics is the scientific study of how gases flow. In motorsports, it is used to study the the flow of air over, under, and around a vehicle as it speeds forward. Designers aim for their vehicle to cut through the air as smoothly as possible without creating disturbances in the airflow, which are known as turbulence. The more smoothly shaped, or streamlined, a vehicle is, the faster it can potentially travel. This is because streamlined shapes create less drag (a force that is caused by the resistance of air, that slows down a moving object). Aerodynamics can have a huge impact on performance,

Diffuser
The diffuser smooths out the flow of air as it exits from underneath the car by helping suck it up and out at high speed.

Underbody
The underbody of an F1 car generates some downforce.

▲ Air moving over a car wing travels faster underneath it than above it. The air pressure below the wing is lower than that above, generating downforce.

especially in high-speed, open-wheel classes such as Champ Cars and F1. Attaching a nonstreamlined radio aerial to the nose of one of these vehicles, for example, could be the same as cutting ten horsepower from its engine power.

The wing of an aircraft generates lift, but car wings (see diagram, above) do the opposite— they help the car "stick" to the ground. A type of wing called a spoiler is attached to the rear of many rally cars and saloon cars. Air is deflected around the spoiler, building up higher air pressure directly in front of it. This generates downforce, which pushes the rear of the car down on the ground. Downforce is essential for maintaining grip and allowing drivers to speed through corners, but it also causes unwanted drag. Because race teams have to strike a delicate balance between drag and downforce, they make adjustments to their car's aerodynamic setup for each circuit.

COMPUTER DESIGN

Engineers and designers of race vehicles use cutting-edge technology to help them. Each component that affects a vehicle's speed goes through many hours of computer-aided design and testing. Aerodynamic features are tested in advanced wind tunnels and by using computer simulation. Computational fluid dynamics, or CFD, is an increasingly powerful tool. It is used to analyze the flow of liquids and gases by computer simulation. CFD can model and test many different parts of a bike or a car; it also acts as a virtual wind tunnel to test how air flows around a moving race vehicle.

AERODYNAMIC INNOVATIONS

Aerodynamic research is heavily funded at the top levels of motorsports, as teams look for even the smallest advantage that will lead to a major difference over the entire length of a race. Not all aerodynamic innovations have been about increasing speed and performance, however; many have been about safety. Roof flaps were introduced to NASCAR in 1994 to prevent cars from becoming airborne during a high-speed spin. The flaps open at the rear of the roof to disrupt the airflow, which decreases lift and helps keep the car on the ground.

▲ This 1967 Chaparral 2F was one of the first racing cars to feature a high wing mounted on thin struts.

◀◀ A sprint car's shape and its light weight mean that at top speeds, aerodynamic lift could flip it up into the air. The giant wing on the roof, however, generates enough downforce to keep the car on the track.

BODYWORK

A race vehicle has to be as aerodynamic as possible, but it must also be built according to competition rules and combine strength, safety, and function. Many saloon- or sedan-based racing cars have a strong tubular frame, often made out of steel, onto which body panels and

other components are attached. This frame supports the vehicle. Many single-seater open-wheel cars have a monocoque body. This is an all-in-one design in which the outer skin supports the weight of the car instead of an internal frame. An advanced monocoque is usually made out of layers of composite materials (materials that are made from two or more different materials). It forms a lightweight but incredibly strong "survival" cell for the driver. A new design must pass extensive safety and crash tests, and researchers are developing further ways to divert more of the force of a crash away from the driver. For example, in NASCAR's Car of Tomorrow, the driver's seat has been moved back and farther into the center of the car to minimize injuries from side impacts.

▲ With its bodywork removed, the monocoque of Ayrton Senna's 1987 Lotus 99T is clearly visible. The main ingredient in an F1 monocoque is carbon fiber—a composite material that is twice as strong as steel, but five times lighter.

Rear wing
Up to one third of the car's downforce can be generated by its rear wing, which also produces significant drag because of its angle.

Barge boards
Barge boards, or turning vanes, help smooth out airflow that has been disrupted by the front wheels. They also separate the airflow into two parts—one is diverted around the car to help reduce drag, the other travels through the sidepods to cool down the engine.

▲ A Formula One car has many aerodynamic features that work as the car races on the track. An IndyCar or F1 car generates so much downforce that it could technically run upside down, sticking to a ceiling, as it raced at more than 124mph (200km/h).

Front wing
The front wing can generate as much as one quarter of the car's downforce. It also directs the air around the car.

ENGINE AND BRAKES

At the core of any winning racing car or bike design is a powerful, efficient, and reliable engine. Almost all racing vehicles use an internal combustion engine to provide power. Heavy-duty brakes are required to bring a fast-moving vehicle to a halt.

▲ A 1927 advertising poster for motor oil celebrates the record-breaking Sunbeam (pictured top)—the first car to travel at more than 200mph (320km/h).

▼ A V8-engine configuration has eight cylinders that are offset in two rows of four, at an angle 60–90° apart. An inline-4, or straight-4, engine has four cylinders in a straight line. A flat-4 engine has four cylinders laid in two rows, 180° apart.

THE ENGINE

There are many types of engines, but in general, most of them ignite a mixture of fuel and air in their cylinders to convert chemical energy into heat energy. This drives a cylinder piston up and down, turning the heat energy into mechanical energy that passes through the transmission system (consisting of a gearbox and some form of driveshaft or drivechain) to send power to the wheels. This process sounds fairly simple, but in reality, racing engines are incredibly complex, precise machines. They are also some of the most highly pushed devices in the world, due to their ultrafast, repeated movements and the phenomenal heat, pressure, and mechanical forces that they experience. Each one of an IndyCar's eight pistons, for example, travels more than one half mile up and down every minute, while at maximum acceleration, the pistons of a Formula One engine may be subjected to forces that are 9,000 times the force of gravity. Given such great stresses, it is no surprise that engine problems cause many of the retirements in motor racing.

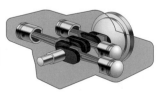

V8   **Inline-4**   **Flat-4**

In some classes of racing, one manufacturer supplies all of the teams with their engines—Zytek engines power all the cars in A1GP, for example, while Honda will supply all IndyCar engines between 2006 and 2009. In other classes, a team forges a partnership with a major engine supplier—as is the case with the McLaren Formula One team and its engine supplier, Mercedes.

Engines are measured in a number of ways, including their configuration (the number and arrangement of their major parts, particularly their cylinders), how much power they generate, and their displacement. Engine displacement is the total volume of air and fuel that an engine can draw into its cylinders during one engine cycle. It is usually measured in cubic centimeters (cc) or liters (one liter equals 1,000cc). A small pocket bike engine may have a displacement of 40–50cc. The mighty 1927 Sunbeam car (see left), on the other hand, boasted not one, but two 22.4-liter engines.

▲ A mechanic works on a three-liter, V12-cylinder Ferrari F1 engine at the British GP in 1995.

MORE POWER

An engine's power output is often measured in horsepower (hp) or brake horsepower (bhp). One hp is equal to around 746 watts. To put engine power into perspective, most family saloon cars generate 70–120hp. A top rally car may generate more than 300hp, while the V12-cylinder engine of the BMW LMR (winner of the 1999 Le Mans 24 Hours) produced more than 590hp. Over the decades, engineers have tried many ways to increase an engine's power. In the early days, engine displacement was considered to be the key. Manufacturers built bigger and bigger engines, regardless of the weight. The 1912 Fiat S76, for example, had a 28.3-liter engine that was so large, the driver had to peer around it to see in front of them. In recent years, engines have become ever smaller, lighter, and more powerful. Engineering advances allow these machines to generate more power by running at faster speeds and by being more efficient at converting the energy that is generated by burning fuel and air in their cylinders into power to drive the race vehicle. Some engines have a turbocharger or supercharger. These devices compress and blow air into the engine to increase the pressure of the

fuel and air mixture, which boosts power. Computerized engine control units (ECUs) are found in many racing vehicles. Sensors monitor the running of the engine and its parts in minute detail, communicating important data to the driver and the race team's base, as well as controlling engine variables such as the amount of fuel that is injected and the timing of the ignition system.

▲ In a disk-braking system, fluid is forced down a tube as the brake pedal is pressed. The fluid forces levers called brake calipers to press brake pads onto a disk that rotates with the wheel.

BRAKING

All of this power and speed needs to be stopped, and quickly. Racing brakes are incredibly powerful. Braking hard in an F1 car can bring it from 124mph (200km/h) to a halt in just 180 feet (55m) and 1.9 seconds. Most racing bikes and cars use brake disks (see diagram). The brake pads generate enormous amounts of friction, which slows down the wheel and car but produces vast quantities of heat. With severe braking, parts of a V8 Supercar's brakes, for example, reach 652°F (900°C). Some vehicles have brake vents that channel cooling air over the brakes. Brake disks are usually made from steel or lighter carbon fiber. In many vehicles, including NASCAR, Formula One, and World Rally Championship cars, drivers can adjust the brake bias—the difference in the amount of force that is applied by the brakes to the front and back wheels. A typical setup has a little more brake force applied to the front wheels because, when braking, weight transfers to the front of the car, allowing harder braking to the front wheels without them locking.

◄◄ The Porsche 917/30 boasted a flat-12 cylinder engine with a displacement of 5.4 liters, generating a maximum of 1,500hp with two turbochargers attached.

▲ Champ Car driver Bruno Junqueira looks on as an engineer changes the brakes on his Newman-Haas Racing Lola in 2003.

◄ Braking heavily, Jarno Trulli locks the front-left wheel of his Honda-engined Jordan F1 car in 2001.

HANDLING AND CONTROL

In order for a racing vehicle to be competitive, it has to be equipped not only with excellent aerodynamics and enough power from its engine, but it must also have responsive controls and be able to grip the track and handle well.

COCKPIT CONTROLS

A driver or rider needs easy access to all of their key controls. Modern electronic aids have made the steering wheel one of the most complex parts of an open-wheel car. It provides all of the key data and controls that a driver needs at their fingertips, including paddle switches for clutch and gear changing. An F1 steering wheel, for example, can consist of 120 parts, take around 100 hours to build, and cost up to $60,000.

SUSPENSION

In simple terms, suspension systems consist of a spring that allows each wheel to move up and down and a shock absorber that controls how much the wheel rebounds. In motorsports, suspension works to keep a vehicle's tires on the road, with the wheels sharing the vehicle's weight as evenly as possible. A good suspension setup helps transmit power to the road and maximize grip. Computer-controlled active suspension is used in many classes, including endurance racing and rallying. It has sensors that feed data about the road and state of the suspension to a computer. This computer constantly adjusts the suspension by controlling the amount of fluid in the cylinders, called hydraulic actuators, that make each spring softer or stiffer.

WHERE RUBBER MEETS ROAD

A lot of hard work, expense, and advanced technology go into producing a vehicle's engine, chassis, and systems, but the power that they generate can only be transmitted to the ground via a surprisingly small area of tire surface. The total area of an IndyCar's four tires that touches the ground at any one moment as it races at more than 186mph (300km/h) is only about the size of a single page from this book. This tiny area must support the weight of the car and the enormous downforce that it creates, provide grip through corners, and generate the forward motion necessary to propel the car at breakneck speeds.

In many classes of motorsports, including NASCAR, Indy racing, and F1, racing tires are wider than regular road tires. They are built to last a few hundred miles (compared to 930 miles, or 15,000km, for a road tire) and are often made from much softer rubber compounds with little or no tread (the pattern of grooves that are in a tire's surface). They tend to work best at high temperatures (194–230°F, or 90–110°C, in the case of F1 dry tires), when they become sticky. These temperatures are only reached when racing at high speeds, although teams assist the process by wrapping electrically heated tire warmers around the tires before they are put on a vehicle.

▲ *An engineer wraps an F1 tire in a tire-warming blanket. Many race tires are inflated with nitrogen or nitrogen-rich air because it reacts less to changing temperatures and humidity than regular air does. This keeps the tire pressure constant, helping the car grip and handle well.*

▶ *The steering wheel of Ralf Schumacher's 2006 Toyota TF106 contains 14 control buttons, four gear-change or clutch paddles, and six adjustable dials.*

Pit con
Sends message to the pits confirming that a message has been received

Data screen
Displays key data such as engine revs, lap time, speed, and gear

Gear-change paddle

Pit-lane speed limiter

Launch control
Used at the start to help a fast getaway without wheelspin

Drink button
Releases fluid through a tube into the driver's helmet

Clutch paddle

TIRE TYPES

In some competitions, teams use treadless tires, or slicks, that offer the maximum amount of surface area that is in direct contact with the track. In difficult track and weather conditions, intermediate or wet-weather tires may be used These have a greater amount of tread, which channels water out from underneath the tire. If water builds up between the road and the tire, a vehicle may lose all of its grip and control. This is known as aquaplaning. Off-road tires have deep, chunky tread patterns that grip loose surfaces and withstand a lot of punishment, while rally drivers choose from a wide range of tires, including studded tires for racing on ice.

VEHICLE HANDLING

When pushing a vehicle to the limit, a racer must be aware of how it handles in different situations. A motorcycle, for example, may be very responsive to changes in direction but difficult to keep moving in a straight line. Some cars have incredible acceleration but are difficult to pull through tight corners. Many different elements determine how well a vehicle handles, but two important ones are understeer or oversteer (see diagram, right).

Understeer can lead to front tire wear and also to the driver having to tackle corners at a slower speed than usual. Some drivers prefer a vehicle that oversteers slightly, because the car feels more responsive. Serious oversteer, however, can cause a car to spin out of control. Teams will sometimes reduce understeer or oversteer by making adjustments to the aerodynamics to increase downforce to one part of the car, or by adjusting the suspension or the alignment of the wheels.

▲ Before the start of a drag race, drivers apply water to their back tires and perform a "burnout." This heats up the tires and makes them sticky, helping them grip the track.

Oversteer occurs when the front wheels grip, but the rear wheels lose traction. The back of the car may start to skew around.

Understeer is when the front wheels lose grip and traction. The car may plow straight ahead at a corner.

▼ Racing drivers are more likely to lose control when the track is wet. This 15-car pileup took place at the 2005 Aaron's 312 Busch Series race, which was delayed by rain.

PREPARATION AND THE PITS

No matter how fast, reliable, and innovative a race team's cars or bikes are, if the team does not get its preparation and setup right and does not perform well in the pits, its race is as good as over.

PREPARATION AND DATA

Professional race teams run many hours of testing, in which they fine-tune their vehicle, establish that it is fast, reliable, and handles well, and make pinpoint adjustments if it is not. Feedback from the driver or rider is usually combined with complex telemetry data that is sent from sensors attached to the race vehicle back to the team's computers. Every element of a car's performance—from tire grip and wear to engine temperature and oil pressure—is analyzed in painstaking detail. Williams' 2004 F1 car, the FW26, featured almost 200 sensors that sent back more than 150,000 measurements per second.

▲ *Patrick Freisacher of the Red Bull Junior team checks telemetry data from his Formula 3000 car during qualifying.*

GETTING THE RIGHT SETUP

Exactly how a bike or car is tuned and prepared to run in a particular race and weather conditions is known as its setup. This can vary greatly from race to race, since adjustments can be made to so many parts of the vehicle—steering and suspension; engine, brakes, and aerodynamic features; as well as tire type and pressure. The number of options can create a real headache. NASCAR engineers, for instance, may have to choose from as many as 120 different types of shock absorbers. In MotoGP, the wheelbase of the bike—the distance between the axles of

each wheel—can be lengthened or shortened. A longer wheelbase, which can improve the bike's stability when it is racing in a straight line, may work best for a high-speed circuit with long straights. A shorter wheelbase makes the bike better at changing its direction quickly, and it may be the best option for a circuit such as Mugello, in Italy, which has many tight turns and chicanes.

THE PITS

In many types of motor racing, competitors take their vehicles off the circuit and into the pit lane to refuel, change tires. and make running repairs. Today, pit activity is precisely choreographed, and strict rules govern safety, pit-lane behavior, and maximum pit-lane speed. A breach of the rules leads to a punishment such as the ten-second stop-and-go penalty, in which a car sits idle with no work allowed on it. A pit stop is timed from when the car or bike comes to a halt and the pit crew leaps into action. A seven-person NASCAR crew can complete a stop in less than 14 seconds. In F1, with unlimited pit crew numbers, stops can be as short as six seconds, depending on the amount of fuel that is added. If major repairs are needed, a stop may last much longer. Since each fraction of a second can make a difference to a driver's race position, pit crews train long and hard.

▲ *During the 2006 Dakar Rally, Robby Gordon and his codriver Darren Skilton repair their Hummer H3 in the desert.*

▲ *A race team's pit crew must be ready to spring into action at any moment. Here, members of Renault's F1 pit crew follow the action at the 2005 Japanese GP on a television monitor.*

PIT-STOP STRATEGIES

Different circuits, race situations, weather, and track conditions can prompt different pit-stop strategies. An F1 pit stop may only take seven seconds, but the total time that is lost by entering and exiting the pit lane can be around 30 seconds. Teams have to weigh the benefits of a pit visit (fresh tires, for example) against the added speed that comes from staying out on the track with less fuel (a heavy fuel load can add up to two seconds to an F1 car's lap time). In 2004, Ferrari and Michael Schumacher surprised opponents with a four-stop strategy for winning the French GP. In endurance racing, pit stops are much more numerous—at the 2003 Le Mans 24 Hours, the Bentley Speed Eight car made 29 stops.

◀ Canada's Ross Bentley takes over as the driver from Freddy Lienhard of Switzerland during a pit stop at the 2000 Daytona 24 Hours endurance race.

▼ Rubens Barrichello's Ferrari pit crew at work (below): the lollipop man (1) directs the car in and holds up a board that reads: "BRAKE"; this is flipped to reveal "1ST GEAR" when the car can leave. Jack men (not pictured) lift the car off the ground. Three men change each wheel: the gun man (2) uses an air gun to loosen and tighten the wheel nuts; one man positions the new tire (3); another takes away the old tire (4). Two men (5, 6) use an aviation fuel hose to refuel. Debris in the sidepods is removed (7, 8); while another pit crewman may clean the driver's visor.

TECHNIQUES AND TACTICS

Regardless of the quality of their vehicle, racers need a wide array of skills and techniques to challenge for victory. They must be able to start fast, choose the right racing lines, negotiate bends and (in some classes) jumps, overtake, and defend a lead. Basic "racecraft"—awareness of how the vehicle is performing and having a strategy to cross the finish line first—is also vital.

FAST STARTS

Getting off to a good start demands sharp focus, quick reactions, awareness of rival racers, and masterful vehicle control. In many forms of track racing, the start is especially important, because it provides the best chance to move up the field on tight circuits with few opportunities for overtaking. Drivers and riders must accelerate as fast as possible, without applying so many revs to the engine that they wheelspin or lose control. As they pull away from a crowded starting grid, racers are on the lookout for gaps into which they can dart ahead of other racers. At the same time, they must be aware of rivals who are defending their position by blocking or cutting off the space.

SMOOTHLY DOES IT

A smooth racing style not only tends to lead to fewer mistakes, but it can be the fastest option overall and may also result in less wear and tear on the vehicle. Drivers and riders focus on smoothly shifting their vehicle's gears up and down (an F1 driver may make more than 2,500 gear changes during a race) as well as careful

▲ *Japan's Toshi Arai uses opposite lock to take his Subaru through a tight corner in the 2005 Rally of New Zealand.*

use of the brakes. Drivers may brake as late and as hard as possible when they are overtaking, for example, but they must avoid locking up the brakes. This stops one or more of the wheels from spinning and can cause a flat spot (serious wear on one part of the tire) or a loss of control that may send the vehicle into a skid.

THE RACING LINE

There are many routes that a rider or driver can take around a track, but there is rarely more than one that is the fastest and most efficient. By the halfway point of the race, that

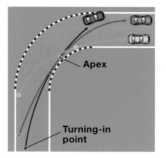

A good racing line (blue) starts from the outside of the track and clips the inside point, or apex, of the turn. An early turn (red) can lead to problems in negotiating the bend. Cautious racers may take a late line (yellow), turning into the corner sharply but at a slow speed.

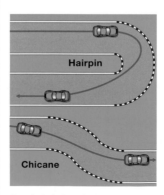

At a hairpin bend, drivers have to brake hard and then turn late. At a chicane, drivers attempt to turn and brake as little as possible.

▲ *Jim Clark, Jackie Stewart, Graham Hill, and Dan Gurney drift around a bend at the 1965 Italian GP.*

▶ *Riders in a 2005 MotoGP race show the changes in body positions that are required to turn left and right to negotiate the curves of a chicane at Japan's Motegi Twin Ring Circuit.*

route is often shown on the track as a darker area that has been left by the tire trails of a heavy stream of traffic. This is called the racing line, and it particularly applies to turns and bends. Three key parts of a racing line are the turn-in point, where the car actually enters the corner, the apex, which is the slowest part of the turn and where the car is closest to the inside of the corner, and the exit point, where the car is back on a straight racing line and can accelerate away. Experienced racers look to brake before entering the corner, when

▲ Doug Dehaan (80) leads a group of riders around a supercross turn. His inside foot is out, in front of his body weight in case he has to dab, or touch the ground with his boot.

they are still traveling on a more or less straight line. This is when braking is most efficient and is less likely to cause any loss of control. Then they try to take the best possible line through the bend and accelerate as their vehicle straightens out on its exit. Entering a corner at too high of a speed or at too early of an apex point can lead to errors. The exact line that a racer takes also depends on the track and weather conditions and whether their vehicle tends to understeer or oversteer (see p. 61). In rallying, drivers sometimes employ an oversteering technique known as opposite lock to quickly get their car through a turn by sliding around the back end of the vehicle.

CORNERING ON TWO WHEELS

Taking a turn on a circuit-racing motorcycle involves the rider shifting their weight and balance as they lean their bike into a bend. With the big machines of MotoGP and Superbikes, the rider's lean angle is so great that they can brush the ground with their knee sliders as they take a tight turn. However, the more a bike leans, the worse its suspension works and the less traction the bike's wheels have with the track surface. So racers try to cut out unnecessary leaning and maintain their stability by holding their lean angle constant as they swoop through a curve and open up the throttle smoothly as they return to a vertical position. In off-road and speedway riding, riders take corners by angling the bike inward, putting their inside foot forward and down, and sliding the back of their bike around the curve.

OVERTAKING

It is possible to move up the field in a race without overtaking, such as when other cars take pit stops, crash out, or retire. In most circumstances, however, overtaking prowess is crucial. In some classes, overtaking simply involves brute power down a long straight. If one car has a lot more engine power and a better setup than the car ahead of it, it may power past before the next turn. Some classes feature innovations to assist overtaking. A "push to pass" button was introduced to Champ Cars in 2004, for example. It releases an extra burst of 50 horsepower to the cars' Ford Cosworth XFE engines, but its use is limited to 60 seconds per race. In NASCAR and other oval-circuit racing, overtaking opportunities can present themselves on the high-speed banked turns. If a car rises up the bank, its driver may need to slow down to keep it under control, giving a chasing driver the chance to take a shorter route around the lead vehicle on the inside of the track. Outbraking an opponent is another way of overtaking. In simple terms, this is when one vehicle brakes later than another as they approach a turn. The late braker hopes to use their speed advantage to get their nose in front of their opponent, claiming the corner and forcing their rival to take a slower line through the turn.

Outbraking is a precise business, however, and errors in judgment can see the overtaker crash, take a poor line into a bend, or collide with another vehicle.

DRAFTING

Drafting (or slipstreaming) is a particular feature of NASCAR races at the giant superspeedway tracks, as well as in some other classes of racing. It occurs when two or more cars or motorcycles race in single file, sharing a pocket of air. In effect, the front car punches a hole through the air, creating a low density pocket of air behind it.

▲ NASCAR driver Junior Johnson was the first to employ the technique of drafting to his advantage during a race.

▼ Brazil's Antonio Pizzonia brakes late, claiming the inside line through the corner and overtaking Rob Nguyen of Australia during a Formula 3000 race in 2002.

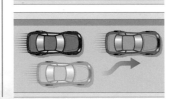

◄ A slingshot maneuver sees the chasing driver use the air pressure behind the lead car to propel him or her forward so that they can pull out. and overtake

This allows the following cars to slip through the air more easily, which uses less engine power and fuel. The front car also benefits, because good drafting enables all of the cars in a draft line to travel a little faster than they would if they raced alone. Drafting can also allow a well-timed overtaking move known as a slingshot. By dropping back from the first car a little, the low-pressure air pocket behind the first car effectively "sucks" the second car forward. The second driver then gains a little more speed as they pull out to the side to pass the first car. Drafting was first employed in 1960 by NASCAR's Junior Johnson, whose Chevrolet was around 9mph (15km/h) slower than his Plymouth-driving rivals. However, Johnson found that he could draft behind the Plymouths to keep up and went on to record a famous Daytona 500 win. Changes to the aerodynamics of modern F1 and some other open-wheel cars means that drafting tends to be less important in these classes.

▲ *Dale Earnhardt, Jr. drafts behind Kyle Busch during the Budweiser Shootout at Daytona International Speedway, Florida, in February 2006.*

DEFENDING A POSITION

In some forms of racing, a skillful driver can stay ahead of an opponent by adopting a defensive driving style. For example, the racer may take a slightly different racing line into bends—one that may not be the fastest line available, but that cuts off the angles for the chasing car to make a passing move on the inside or outside. In many classes of motorsports, there are strict rules on what defensive moves are allowed. In Formula One, for example, a driver is only allowed to change their line going into a corner once. Weaving back and forth across the

track to protect a race position is classified as illegal blocking. Drivers defending their position may also make use of backmarkers that they are about to lap. If the first car overtakes a backmarker just before a turn, their rival may get stuck behind the slow backmarker for a crucial period. The front vehicle can then build up a lead. Encountering backmarkers, however, can also give the chasing car a chance, as it slows down the lead car and may make an unexpected move possible. This was seen in dramatic fashion at the 2000 Belgian GP where, as Michael Schumacher went to pass backmarker Ricardo Zonta on the left, Mika Hakkinen pulled a stunning move, diving for the right to get ahead of both cars and going on to win the race.

RACING STRATEGY

Rarely is top-class racing as simple as putting the accelerator pedal to the floor and driving as quickly and as aggressively as possible from the starting grid to the finish line. In many forms of racing, drivers must choose when to push their vehicle as hard as they can and when not to in order to conserve fuel and minimize wear on the engine, tires, and brakes. Pit-stop, overtaking, and drafting strategies may all play a major part in

race tactics, as can rivals crashing out or the appearance of the safety car or a caution flag. Concentration to the very end of the race is essential, since after many hours and miles of racing, the difference between winning and losing can be less than a car's length. The average race-winning margin in Formula One in 2005 was 12.3 seconds. In 2002, the IndyCar race at Chicagoland saw first and second place separated by a microscopic 0.0024 seconds!

◄◄ *Second-placed Russell Ingall overtakes and laps 13th-placed Greg Murphy during the Bob Jane T Marts 1000 V8 Supercar race at Bathurst, Australia, in October 2002.*

▲ *In one of the closest-ever finishes, Dan Wheldon beats Helio Castroneves (second) by just 0.014 seconds in the Peak Antifreeze Indy 300 at Chicagoland, Illinois, in September 2005. Sam Hornish, Jr. came in third.*

A RACER'S LIFE

Early racers did not give much thought to their physical and mental health. Today, in order to achieve success at the top, drivers and riders need to be highly-trained and disciplined athletes in order to withstand the extraordinary demands on their bodies and minds that are created by the physical extremes of racing.

ALBERT PARK

14 (2.1G)
13 (1.9G)
15 (2.5G)
12 (3.4G)
16 (1.7G)
9 (2G)
11 (3G)
17 (2.4G)
10 (2.8G)
8 (2.6G)
7 (1.6G)
6 (2.1G)
1 (2.1G)
2 (2.4G)
5 (3.1G)
4 (2.3G)
3 (1.6G)

A FULL BODY WORKOUT

All forms of racing place stresses on the body, and the faster a driver travels, the greater the stresses are. In IndyCar or Formula One racing, for example, drivers may be jerked from a stationary position to around 99mph (160km/h) in less than four seconds. Sharp braking can bring them back to a standstill in less than three seconds.

A driver's body—especially the neck muscles— is subjected to intense forces during acceleration and deceleration and when taking bends and corners at high speeds. Braking hard to take the Imola Circuit's tight Acque Minerali corner, for example, can lead to drivers experiencing more than 4.1G. This is 4.1 times the normal gravitational force that we feel on Earth—in effect, the force is 4.1 times their own body weight. At such high g-forces (G), it takes great strength to maintain control and keep the head upright with a force of 88 lbs. (40kg) or more pulling it to one side. Peripheral vision can also be distorted with high g-forces. In 2001, a CART race at the Texas Motor Speedway saw drivers experience almost 5Gs during turns and was called off after some racers reported dizziness. The huge amounts of downforce that are generated by Formula One cars effectively increases the vehicle's weight to 1.25 tons, while even the smoothest of circuits and most secure of racing harnesses will see drivers suffer some degree of buffeting and knocks to their body.

At rest, a normal person's heart rate will be around 60–80 beats per minute. When racing, a driver's heart rate can rise to between 180 and 210 beats per minute. Put simply, racers need to be incredibly healthy and strong in order to be able to perform. They maintain their all-around fitness levels through running, swimming, cycling, and other similar exercises; they also build up their muscle strength to withstand the forces during a race.

RACE CLOTHING

Many early racers did not wear helmets, while Jim Clark often wore a cardigan, and Mike Hawthorn wore a bow tie when racing. Race clothing is very different today. Advances in material technology has created astonishing flame-proof clothing such as that made from Nomex cloth. Nomex suits used in Indy racing, for example, protect the wearer against fires as hot as 1,292°F (700°C) for up to 12 seconds. Advertising patches and logos also have to conform to strict safety standards. Underneath their outer suit, racers wear socks, long-johns-styled underwear, and T-shirts, also made out of Nomex, along with custom race boots and Nomex-covered gloves with a thin leather or sticky palm to enable the driver to feel the wheel as much as possible. On top of their clothing will be a fireproof balaclava and an advanced crash helmet (see p. 70).

DIET, NUTRITION, AND FLUID INTAKE

Racers monitor their food and drink intake throughout the year, but especially in the periods leading up to and during race weekends. Most top drivers and riders consume pasta and other carbohydrate-rich foods in order to provide energy to increase their stamina.

▲ *Australia's Albert Park Circuit has 17 turns. In the 2006 F1 GP, these had to be navigated 58 times in the race. This map shows the g-forces (G, in brackets) that a driver experiences at each corner.*

◄◄ *Formula One driver Kimi Räikkönen stays in shape by working out in the gym.*

▼ *A driver's racewear usually consists of fire-resistant underwear (right) covered by a full race suit, gloves, boots, and a helmet.*

With high summer temperatures and the tremendous exertion that is involved in high-speed racing, temperatures can reach as high as 122°F (50°C) inside of the racing suit. Fluid loss can see a driver lose as much as 7 lbs. (3kg) during a Formula One race, for example. Dehydration can cause a loss of mental and physical sharpness and is something that all racers look to avoid. At the 1982 Brazilian GP, Nelson Piquet crossed the finish line first but was so dehydrated that he could not celebrate on the podium and had to be treated by medical staff.

MENTAL DEMANDS

While the life of a top racer may appear to be glamorous, it is a role that demands great responsibility. As the public face and focal point of an entire race team, a racer has to maintain a good public image with the fans and the media, meet with sponsors, and perform a number of other team duties. A physically-fit, healthy, and focused racer is more able to take on the incredible amount of technical information that is provided by their race team during testing, preparation, qualifying, and racing. The information, however, needs to flow both ways, and drivers and riders who are able to give precise technical feedback to their team's engineers and strategists are a great asset. In addition to overtaking or defending their position, drivers have to follow pit-lane instructions and deal with large amounts of data and make many split-second decisions concerning their vehicle, distances, speeds, racing conditions, and the circuit that they are racing on. Each feature of a

track imposes enormous physical forces on a racer. They also provide a severe mental test of memory, hand-eye coordination, nerves, and judgment. At the same time, the racer has to contend with the prospect that one slip in concentration or a small error in judgment could result in a crash and bring with it the possibility of severe injuries or death.

▲ A fatigued Jeff Gordon rests after winning the NASCAR Winston Cup Global Crossing at the Glen race in 2001.

▶ At the 1994 German GP, four mechanics were engulfed by a fireball when fuel spilled over Jos Verstappen's Benetton during a pit stop. Thanks to their Nomex clothing, no one was seriously injured.

◀ Daniel Carlsson takes a drink during the Rally of Norway. The FIA recommends that drivers drink one liter of water or fruit juice before, two liters during, and two liters after a race.

RACE SAFETY

Motor racing may be a dangerous sport, but in the last ten years or so, it has taken safety issues increasingly seriously. The focus is on the protection of the driver and rider through improved racewear, vehicle design, safer circuits, and efficient marshaling and race rules.

▲ SAFER (Steel and Foam Energy Reduction) barriers, which absorb energy from a crash and reduce the impact on the driver, have been installed at most IRL and many NASCAR tracks.

SAFETY INNOVATIONS

Different classes of racing and vehicles have different safety features, from the cutout cords that are worn around the wrist of a speedway rider to kill the engine in an emergency to roll cages and window netting in NASCARs and rally cars to protect drivers in the event of a crash and roll. In-depth research, advanced materials, and the use of computer simulation to model crash conditions and other problem areas has led to several new safety initiatives. Crash testing of prototype models has been made more rigorous, while F1 drivers are drilled to escape from the cockpit in less than ten seconds. NASCARs now feature windshields made out of Lexan—a soft but strong and hard-to-shatter polycarbonate that is used for the canopies of fighter planes. In 2000, the Indy Racing League (IRL)

introduced collapsible steering wheel columns that telescope down on impact. Accident data recorders have also been installed in all IRL cars. The HANS (Head and Neck Support) devices, developed by American Bob Hubbard, have become compulsory in many forms of racing, including Champ Cars, Formula One since 2003, and the World Rally Championship since 2005.

HEAD PROTECTION

Compared to the "hard hats" of the 1950s, a modern full-face race helmet is incredibly advanced. The smallest, softest piece of debris becomes lethal if it comes into contact with a vehicle traveling at more than 124mph (200km/h), so modern helmets are built to be able to withstand incredible forces of impact. They are constructed from several layers, including a hard, lightweight outer shell, a Nomex lining that absorbs sweat and draws away heat from the head but repels fire, and a series of pads that provide protection and ensure a perfect fit. In many classes of motorsports, helmets are complex devices that feature ventilation systems with filters to prevent small particles of track debris from entering the helmet, a fluid delivery system to the driver via a small tube, as well as an embedded microphone and earpieces for two-way radio communications. The visor may be specially treated to resist glare and fogging and may come complete with a small number of

▼ *This cutaway diagram of a modern Indy racing helmet shows the many advanced safety features that protect a driver's head in the event of an accident.*

▼ Marshals assist Khalil Beschir after his car flipped over during the inaugural A1GP race at Brands Hatch, U.K., in 2005.

▲ The HANS device is made out of Kevlar and carbon fiber. Its aim is to prevent the head from snapping sharply in one direction during a crash.

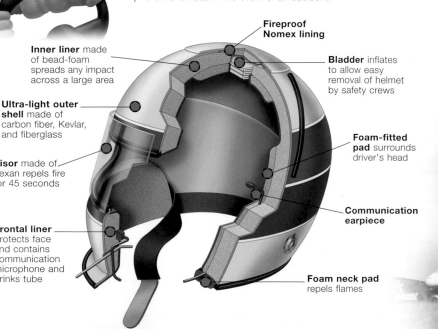

Fireproof Nomex lining

Inner liner made of bead-foam spreads any impact across a large area

Bladder inflates to allow easy removal of helmet by safety crews

Ultra-light outer shell made of carbon fiber, Kevlar, and fiberglass

Foam-fitted pad surrounds driver's head

Visor made of Lexan repels fire for 45 seconds

Communication earpiece

Frontal liner protects face and contains communication microphone and drinks tube

Foam neck pad repels flames

clear tear-off strips that can be removed once they are dirty to ensure maximum visibility. In open-wheel racing and motorcycling, helmets also play an important part in the aerodynamics of the vehicle. IndyCar helmets, for example, have an aerodynamic plate attached that helps create downforce to keep the helmet securely in place. They are also designed with a bladder in the top of the helmet that can be inflated by a small gas cartridge, allowing the helmet to be removed gently without any pressure on potentially injured neck muscles.

SPEED LIMITS

Today's top race vehicles have the potential to go much faster than the motorsports' authorities deem to be safe, so speeds are managed or reduced in a number of ways. Many open-wheel racing circuits have been redesigned to make them safer in general, with larger run-off areas, barriers that spread the impact of a crash and protect the spectators, and additional chicanes and other track features that slow down vehicles. In some competitions, the authorities have introduced rules to limit the engine size and aerodynamic features. Other technical limits that reduce speed include restrictor plates (see p. 30). Attached to karts and NASCARs for certain races, these devices limit the amount of air and fuel that can enter the engine's cylinders, cutting back the vehicle's acceleration and top speed.

MARSHALS

Marshals are track staff at a race, whether that is a rally, off-road competition, or an event on a circuit, who help with its smooth running and safety. Marshals perform a wide range of jobs, including warning drivers about dangers ahead and keeping spectators out of harm's way. When an accident occurs, safety teams must work skillfully and rapidly. It can be a matter of life and death, and many drivers owe their lives to safety crews. Fires must be extinguished or prevented, injured racers or others must be treated on the spot—usually by a doctor—or carefully removed from the crash scene and taken for medical treatment. The vehicle and any debris must be removed safely from the racing area. Marshals on circuits are usually in communication with, and answerable to, the race director. The director makes crucial decisions, such as whether a race should be called off or stopped or, in many competitions, if the safety car should be called out. Safety-car rules vary between different classes, but usually its appearance sees the entire field slow down, stop overtaking, and follow the safety car around until it enters the pits and regular racing can resume.

▲ An F1 safety team practices removing a Sauber team member from the car before the 2002 Canadian GP in Montreal.

▼ Race marshals remove F1 driver Jarno Trulli's Toyota from the track after a collision with Takuma Sato's BAR at the 2005 Japanese GP.

◀ At the 1999 San Marino
GP, a trackside tribute
commemorates
five years since Ayrton
Senna's final race.

▲ Ayrton Senna speeds to
pole position in his Williams
FW16 during qualifying for
the 1994 San Marino GP.

AYRTON SENNA'S LAST RACE

Ayrton Senna started the 1994 San Marino GP at Imola as he had also started the previous two races of the season—in pole position. His mood was quiet, however, following the death of Roland Ratzenberger during practice—the first F1 fatality for 12 years. Senna had tucked an Austrian flag inside of his Williams vehicle, planning to wave it in memory of Ratzenberger at the end of the race. But entering the Tamburello corner on lap five, Senna left the track at more than 186mph (300km/h), hit a wall, and died. The outpouring of emotion was enormous, particularly in Senna's homeland of Brazil, where around one million people attended his funeral. The accident led to controversy, conspiracy theories, and long-running legal action. It also prompted greater research into safety and the modification of many circuits, including Imola, where the high-speed Tamburello is now a slower, safer chicane.

TRACKS AND RACES

Over the last 100 years, motor races have been held in every setting imaginable—from the searing desert temperatures of the Dakar Rally to the glitz and glamour of the Monaco Grand Prix—the jewel of the Formula One season.

▼*Jarno Trulli's F1 Toyota speeds past Suzuka's famous roller coaster in 2005.*

SUZUKA, JAPAN

Suzuka started life as a test track for Honda in 1962 and debuted as a Formula One venue in 1987. It is Japan's foremost racing circuit and one of the toughest tests in the world for a driver. The current track measures just over 3.6 miles (5.8km), contains 18 turns, and crosses over itself just after the Degner Curve. Fans flock to events as varied as Formula Nippon, the annual 620-mile (1,000km) GT Enduro, and rounds of MotoGP. Often held as either the penultimate or last race of the season, the Japanese F1 GP has determined several world titles. Dramatic encounters have included the legendary tussles between Ayrton Senna and Alain Prost in 1989 and 1990.

SUZUKA

Spoon Curve
Degner Curve
Dunlop Curve
Hairpin
"S" Curve
Casino Chicane
First Curve

RALLY OF SWEDEN

An international Rally of Sweden was held in 1950, and in 1965, the event was promoted to a winter rally. Mostly raced on snow, the Rally of Sweden is the coldest World Rally Championship event. Temperatures drop to as low as –17°F (–27°C), posing unique problems for drivers and vehicles. The use of skinny tires that are covered in studs means that cars can cut through the snow at astonishing speeds. In 2003, competitors reached an average speed of 73mph (118km/h), making it the second-fastest WRC event behind the Rally of Finland. To complete its stages successfully, drivers need lightning-quick reactions and intense levels of concentration, as well as the ability to lean their cars into the snowbanks to guide them around corners. France's Sebastian Loeb is the only nonScandinavian driver to have won the rally, in 2004.

▼ *With a variety of codrivers, Swedish legend Stig Blomqvist has won the Rally of Sweden a record of seven times—including this victory in 1973.*

SPA-FRANCORCHAMPS, BELGIUM

One of the finest tracks in the world, Belgium's historic Spa-Francorchamps Circuit opened in 1924. It held 18 Grand Prix between 1950 and 1970, before being dramatically altered and shortened for its return to F1 racing in 1983. The 4.3-mile (6.976km) track retains many famous features, including the uphill Eau Rouge bend, La Source hairpin, and its winding route through the Ardennes forest. Michael Schumacher has won at Spa six times, Ayrton Senna five times, and Jim Clark four times. The circuit is also used for touring cars and sports-endurance racing.

▲ *The BRM P261s of Graham Hill and Jackie Stewart lead the field through Spa's majestic Eau Rouge in 1965.*

SPA-FRANCORCHAMPS

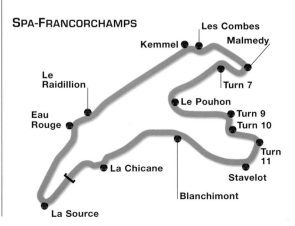

Les Combes
Malmedy
Kemmel
Turn 7
Le Raidillion
Le Pouhon
Eau Rouge
Turn 9
Turn 10
Turn 11
Stavelot
La Chicane
Blanchimont
La Source

▶ Great Britain's Dan Wheldon leads the field at the 2005 Indy 500. He went on to win both the race and the IRL Championship.

INDIANAPOLIS

Turn 3   Back stretch   Turn 2

Road course

Turn 4   Pit straight   Turn 1

INDIANAPOLIS MOTOR SPEEDWAY, U.S.

This world famous 2.5-mile (4.023-km) -long oval was opened in 1909, but its surface of crushed rock and tar proved to be deadly. A new track was laid by embedding 3.2 million bricks in sand and mortar, giving the circuit its nickname—"the Brickyard." Most of the bricks remain beneath the now asphalt surface, with a single "yard of bricks" left exposed at the start/finish line. The first 500-mile (805km) race at the circuit was held in 1911, and the Indy 500, as it became known, was soon one of the world's leading motorsports events. From 1950 to 1960, the Indy 500 counted as one round of the Formula One World Championship. F1 returned to Indianapolis in 2000 with a specially constructed road course. Mostly set inside of the oval, it also uses the pit straight and turn one. NASCAR arrived in 1994 with the highly popular Brickyard 400.

SANTA POD RACEWAY, U.K.

In the late 1960s, a 0.74-mile (1.2-km) -long section of the main runway of Podington airfield was converted into a drag strip. The raceway was named after the airfield, as well as the legendary Santa Ana drag strip in southern California. Now the home of British dragster racing, Santa Pod Raceway holds more than 50 events every year. These included the first and last rounds of the FIA European Drag Racing Championship in 2005. At the other end of the scale, "Run What You Bring" events attract amateurs who race their own vehicles.

▲ Great Britain's Gordon Appleton waits for the green light during the European Drag Racing finals at Santa Pod, U.K., in September 2003.

CIRCUIT VAN DRENTHE

Haarbocht

Geert
Timmer
Bocht

Strubben

Meeuwenmeer

Ruskenhoek

Duikersloot

De Bult

Stekkenwal

Mandeveen

ASSEN, THE NETHERLANDS

At 3.72 miles (5.997km) long, following a series of modifications in 2005, the Circuit van Drenthe at Assen is the longest track in the MotoGP calendar. Since the circuit was built in 1949, it has held one round of the Motorcycle World Championship every year—the only venue in the world to have done so.

Home to the famous Dutch TT event, it is one of the few major road circuits that is designed specifically for motorcycle racing. The technically challenging track, with its steeply banked curves and a surface that offers excellent grip, is also lightning fast, despite having no long straights. It is a favorite with both riders and fans, the latter flocking in their tens of thousands to watch the Dutch TT and several other national and international motorcycle races, including endurance events, motorcycle and sidecar competitions, and, since 1992, the Dutch round of the World Superbike Championship.

THE DAKAR RALLY

The ultimate off-road race, the Dakar Rally was first run in 1979, and for many years, it was known as the Paris to Dakar Rally. Since the mid 1990s, the race organizers have varied the start and end points of the rally. In 1992, it ran to Cape Town, South Africa; in 1994, it ran from Paris to Dakar in Senegal and back again; in 2003, the race ran from Marseille, France, to Sharm El Sheikh in Egypt. Vehicles race in three main categories: motorcycles, large trucks, and automobiles, the latter consisting of cars, buggies, and vans. Almost four fifths of those competing are amateurs, but all entrants must contend with the harsh North African climate and incredibly tough terrain—from rocky plains to mud and sand dunes—which sap the concentration and stamina of everyone except for the toughest competitor.

▲ The Tatra truck of Tomas Tomecek, Jaromir Martinec, and Andre de Azevedo hurtles over a jump during the 2004 Dakar Rally.

▲ Japan's Hiroshi Masuoka passes a camel caravan in the desert during the 2001 Dakar Rally—a classic image of one of the world's greatest endurance races.

NÜRBURGRING
NORDSCHLEIFE

NÜRBURGRING, GERMANY

Germany's first permanent circuit was comprised of a test track and a larger section—the famous Nordschleife. Opening in 1927, the Nordschleife measured a massive 14 miles (22.67km) long and was full of sharp rises and tight bends through forests and mountains. With a reputation as the most demanding circuit of all, it hosted many German F1 Grand Prix. However, calls for greater safety reached a climax in 1976 with the near-fatal crash of Niki Lauda (see p. 102), and the race disappeared from the F1 calendar. A new, shorter, and tamer circuit debuted in the mid 1980s, and it has been the home of the European GP since 1995. Members of the public can drive a modified Nordschleife, which is also used as a test track and as the venue of the annual 24 Hours of Nürburgring, which attracts more than 200,000 spectators.

MONZA, ITALY

A flat, fast track where engine horsepower and raw speed can dominate, Monza is one of the oldest and most evocative circuits in motorsports. Its first Italian GP was all the way back in 1922, after 3,500 construction workers had built the track in only six months. At the time, Monza consisted of a speed course and a road circuit

that were sometimes combined to form a six-mile (10-km) -long lap, but a series of modifications over the years now means that the Grand Prix track measures 3.6 miles (5.79km). The circuit has produced more than its fair share of triumphs and tragedies, as epitomized by the talented Swedish F1 driver Ronnie Peterson. A three-time winner at the circuit, he died there after a crash in 1978. The track also claimed the lives of F1's Jochen Rindt, motorcycle world champion Jarno Saarinen, and, in 1961, Baron Wolfgang von Trips and 14 spectators. Used for sports car racing, the Le Mans Series, and the World Touring Car Championship, Monza is also the fastest circuit in the World Superbike calendar, with average lap speeds in excess of 118mph (190km/h).

◄◄ Jackie Stewart roars past spectators at the Nürburgring during the 1969 German GP.

MONZA

▼ Juan Pablo Montoya leads the pack through the Rettifilio chicane during the 2005 Italian GP at Monza.

DAYTONA INTERNATIONAL SPEEDWAY, U.S.

Daytona is best known as the home of NASCAR's greatest race, the Daytona 500. The 2.5-mile (4-km) -long tri-oval track opened in 1959 and hosted the first-ever Daytona 500 the same year. The NASCAR season opener has often been highly eventful, with brawls between drivers, controversy, high-speed crashes, and spectacular racing. In 1978, for example, Bobby Allison powered through the field from a lowly 33rd place on the grid to win his first Daytona 500. The Speedway site also hosts rounds of Grand-Am, kart, and AMA Superbike racing, as well as the Daytona 24 Hours.

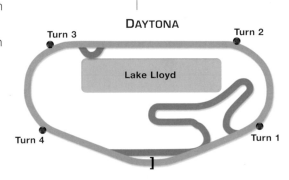

DAYTONA

MONACO

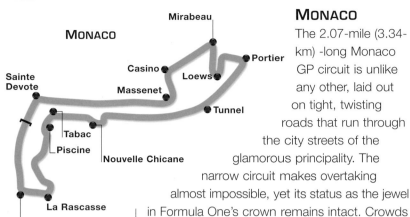

The 2.07-mile (3.34-km) -long Monaco GP circuit is unlike any other, laid out on tight, twisting roads that run through the city streets of the glamorous principality. The narrow circuit makes overtaking almost impossible, yet its status as the jewel in Formula One's crown remains intact. Crowds love the sight of cars powering past glitzy hotels and the yacht-crammed harbor and out of the tunnel at a top race speed of around 150mph (240km/h). First run in 1929 (see pp. 84–85), the Monaco GP has been one round in every World Championship since 1955. Many top drivers, such as Ayrton Senna, Michael Schumacher, and Graham Hill, have relished the circuit's challenge, which requires intense concentration and frequent gear changes. Although qualifying on the front row is deemed essential to win, many cars do not finish, and a well-judged drive can often earn points. In 1996, for example, Olivier Panis started 14th on the grid but was the first of only four cars to finish the race.

▶▶ *A motorcycle and sidecar combination get airborne as they cross Ballaugh Bridge during the 1970 Isle of Man sidecar TT race.*

▲ *Marco Werner in his Audi R8 during the 12 Hours of Sebring in 2005. Werner and his teammates, J. J. Lehto and Tom Kristensen, went on to win the race.*

SEBRING, U.S.

Located in the state of Florida, Sebring opened in 1950 and has only hosted one U.S. Formula One Grand Prix—the very first, in 1959, was won by Bruce McLaren. It is world famous for its endurance race, the 12 Hours of Sebring, which was first held in 1952 and has been run every year since, with the exception of 1974. The circuit's bumpy conditions and hot climate push cars' reliability to the limit. Porsche vehicles have won the most races (17), with the Audi R8 dominating in recent years, with six victories in

a row. The list of winners of the 12 Hours reads like a who's who of racing legends, including Stirling Moss, A. J. Foyt, Bobby Rahal, Tom Kristensen, and three-time winners Phil Hill and Mario Andretti. The great Juan Manuel Fangio won twice at Sebring, as did his nephew, Juan Manuel Fangio II.

ISLE OF MAN TT, U.K.

The Isle of Man is home to one of the most daunting and famous motorcycle races of all—the Isle of Man Tourist Trophy (TT). The first TT race was in 1907; four years later, the famous Snaefell Mountain course was used for the first time. With some adjustments, this is the course that is used today. The 37.6-mile (60.6km) lap winds its way across the island on twisting, and often, narrow lanes and streets, with the threat of buildings and stone walls always present. Part of the Motorcycle World Championship between 1949 and 1975, the course has taken the lives of almost 180 people. The TT had a memorable year in 2004, with new lap records set in many classes, including sidecar, 125cc, and Formula One. In the latter class, John McGuinness set a new overall lap record for the course at 17 minutes, 43.8 seconds—an average speed in excess of 126mph (204km/h).

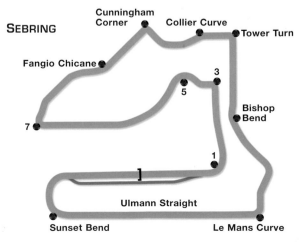

▲ Mirco Baldacci prepares to power his Fiat Punto around one of the many sharp hairpin bends of the Monte Carlo Rally, during round one of the 2003 Junior World Rally Championship.

MONTE CARLO RALLY

The Monte Carlo Rally boasts the longest pedigree of any rally event. First raced in 1911, its early years were open to any type of car. Today, as part of the World Rally Championship, Monte Carlo remains a harsh test of a driver's skill, with roads winding up and down the southern Alps and a range of surfaces, including wet and dry tarmac, snow, and ice to contend with. Sometimes, snow is thrown onto the course by thrill-hungry spectators who flock to the rally, in particular to see the Turini stage that rises up 4,600 feet (1,400m) and includes more than 30 hairpin bends in its 20-mile (32km) length. Three drivers have won four Monte Carlo rallies: Walter Röhrl, Sandro Munari, and Tommi Makinen (with four in a row from 1999). The 2006 event was won by Finland's Marcus Gronholm in a Ford Focus RS WRC.

PIKES PEAK
INTERNATIONAL HILL CLIMB, U.S.

Part of the Rocky Mountains in Colorado, Pikes Peak stands 1,4402 feet (4,391m) high and is the location of the most famous hill climb event in motorsports. The 12.38-mile (19.96km) race is held on a narrow, often gravel, two-lane road. Drivers and riders climb up around 5,000 feet (1,500m) along its length, contending with blind curves and 157 corners without guardrails. It first ran in 1916, when Rea Lentz in a Romano Special won in a time of 20 minutes, 55.6 seconds. Today, various vehicles compete, from open-wheel racers to quad bikes and historic vehicles. The current race record, set in 1994 by Rod Millen, stands at ten minutes, 4.06 seconds.

▲ John Johnson takes a gravelly bend during the 1998 Pikes Peak International Hill Climb.

▲ Ryo Fukuda of Team Japan leads an international field during the first-ever A1GP, held at Brands Hatch, U.K., in September 2005.

BRANDS HATCH, U.K.

A circuit associated with Superbikes, Formula Ford, and sports cars, Brands Hatch was first used for grass-track racing in 1926. The Grand Prix circuit (now 2.6 miles, or 4.19km, long) was built in 1959. Among its features are the infamous Druids hairpin and the plunging Paddock Hill bend. From 1964, Brands Hatch shared the British GP with Silverstone, but the circuit's Formula One swan song came in 1986 with a victory for Nigel Mansell in a Williams car. Since then, the track has had a number of different owners, before becoming part of the Motorsport Vision group (headed by former F1 driver Jonathan Palmer) in 2004. The following year saw Brands Hatch host the opening round of the first A1GP season, while a round of Germany's DTM touring car championship was held there in 2006.

Hawthorn Bend
Westfield Bend
Dingle Dell
Pilgrims Drop
Dingle Dell Corner
Stirlings Bend
Druids
Hailwood Hill
Surtees
Clark Curve
Paddock Hill Bend
Brabham

BRANDS HATCH

▶ Renault driver Fernando Alonso gives a victory wave as he crosses the Nevers Magny-Cours finish line at the end of the 2005 French GP.

BAJA 1,000, MEXICO

The Baja 1,000 was first run in 1967 and is considered to be possibly the toughest of all off-road races. Held in Mexico on the Baja California peninsula, the desert route has changed over the years, but since 2000, it has always started in Ensenada. The tough terrain and conditions prove to be an incredible challenge for the entrants, who compete in different classes for bikes, cars, and trucks. Previous winners include such legends as Parnelli Jones, motocross great Malcolm Smith, and Larry Roeseler—the latter a 14-time winner on two and four wheels. The Baja 1,000 continues to attract famous drivers and riders. In 2004, movie legend and motorsports enthusiast Paul Newman became its oldest entrant at the age of 80.

▶ NASCAR's Robby Gordon competes in the 1990 Baja 1,000 in his BF Goodrich off-road vehicle.

NEVERS MAGNY-COURS, FRANCE

Nevers Magny-Cours was famous for its race school, the Ecole de Pilotage Winfield, before it was transformed into a Grand Prix circuit in the late 1980s. The home of the French GP since 1991, the 2.6-mile (4.2-km) -long circuit has few overtaking points and one of the smoothest track surfaces in F1 racing, making tire choice, car setup, and pit-stop strategies absolutely vital. At the 2004 Grand Prix, for example, Michael Schumacher triumphed after making four pit stops. The circuit also hosts rounds of the World Touring Car and World Superbike championships.

NEVERS MAGNY-COURS

Adelaide
Turn 10
Château d'Eau
Nürburgring
Imola
Golf Course
Lycée
Turn 14
Grande Courbe
Estoril

HOCKENHEIM, GERMANY

Hockenheim has been through several redesigns since being built as a Mercedes test track in 1939. From the early 1960s, the track was used extensively by sports cars and Formula racing below F1. Safety concerns at the Nürburgring saw it host the German GP in 1970, and, since 1977, it has held the event every year except 1985. The latest redesign occurred in time for the 2002 German GP. The long straights that used to race through dense forests were shortened in favor of tight corners. The current 2.83-mile (4.57-km) -long track still retains its famous Moto, or Autodrom, section, where the track twists and turns in front of the giant grandstands that, since Michael Schumacher has been racing, tend to be packed. The new redesign added four more grandstands, bringing the circuit's capacity up to 120,000.

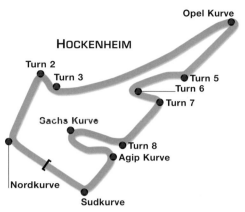

HOCKENHEIM

Opel Kurve
Turn 2
Turn 3
Turn 5
Turn 6
Turn 7
Sachs Kurve
Turn 8
Agip Kurve
Nordkurve
Sudkurve

▲ Luciano Burti's Prost F1 car flips spectacularly into the air at the start of the 2001 German GP at Hockenheim. The Brazilian was unhurt and switched to a spare car for the restart.

LAGUNA SECA, U.S.

Now known as the Mazda Raceway, Laguna Seca was built in 1957 and is one of the United States' premier race tracks. Located in a natural bowl, the 2.2-mile (3.6-km) -long track contains 11 turns and is known for its flowing curves, rises, and falls along its length. The most famous of the circuit's turns are turn 11, the slowest on the circuit, and the Corkscrew chicane at turn 8. Both have seen some outstanding race action, such as Alex Zanardi overtaking Bryan Herta coming out of the Corkscrew chicane on the last lap to win a 1996 CART race. The circuit is home to a wide range of racing, including the American Le Mans Series (ALMS), MotoGP, and the U.S. AMA Superbike Series. In March 2006, the circuit played host to the American round of the inaugural A1GP season.

◄ Nicky Hayden races up the back section of Laguna Seca during the 2005 U.S. MotoGP race. The Honda rider led from the start to the finish line to claim the first MotoGP victory of his career.

Turn 6
The Corkscrew
Rahal Straight
Rainey Curve
Turn 5
Turn 10
Turn 4
Turn 11
Turn 3
Andretti Hairpin
LAGUNA SECA
Turn 1

SILVERSTONE, U.K.

In May 1950, King George VI was present at Silverstone for the first race of the Formula One World Championship, won by eventual world champion Giuseppe Farina. After sharing the race with Aintree (in the 1950s and early 1960s) and then Brands Hatch (from 1964), Silverstone has held the British GP every year since 1987. The circuit is used for many classes of racing, including touring cars and Superbikes, and its track can be set up for seven different layouts. The longest—the Grand Prix layout—is 3.19 miles (5.14km) and features a range of slow and fast corners, chicanes, and a high-speed stretch between Chapel and Stowe, where cars reach more than 186mph (300km/h). The aging circuit's GP status has been under threat in recent years, with poor access causing traffic jams and heavy rain turning car parks into quagmires. In 2004, however, Silverstone's short-term future was assured with a deal to host the British GP until 2009.

▲ The Mini Cooper Challenge is one of a range of motorsports events held at Silverstone.

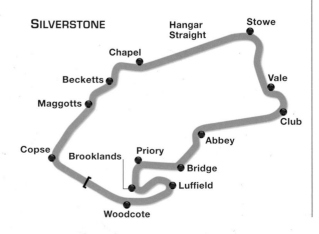

SILVERSTONE

◄ With Michael Schumacher close behind, Fernando Alonso rides a kerb at Imola during the 2005 San Marino GP.

IMOLA, ITALY

The Autodromo Enzo e Dino Ferrari, known as Imola (the name of the neighboring Italian town), was inaugurated in 1953 and has been the home of the San Marino GP since 1981. The three-mile (4.9-km) -long circuit holds Superbike, endurance, and GP2 races, but the spiritual home of Ferrari is best known for its lively atmosphere on F1 weekends. Imola is also one of the few European tracks that runs in a counterclockwise direction. Tragically, it will always be linked to the deaths of Roland Ratzenberger and Ayrton Senna in 1994. Ironically, Senna had recorded eight pole positions at the track (1985–1991 and 1994).

Rivazza
Traguardo
Tamburello
Variante Alta
Acque Minerali
Villeneuve
Piratella
IMOLA
Tosa

TALLADEGA SUPERSPEEDWAY, U.S.

The fastest and longest track in NASCAR, the Talladega Superspeedway began life in 1969 as the Alabama International Motor Speedway. The 2.65-mile (4.28-km) -long track, with three straights and steep banking, allows drivers to reach incredible speeds. In 1987, Bill Elliot recorded an average race speed of just over 211mph (340km/h)—a record for a stock car at any track. Restrictor plates (see p. 30) have since limited cars' top speed, yet Mark Martin managed an average of 187mph (301km/h) in 1997. The track has a reputation for exciting races—during a NASCAR race in 1984, for example, the lead changed hands a staggering 75 times.

▼ Dale Earnhardt, Jr. and Elliott Sadler crash out of the UAW Ford 500, one of two NASCAR Nextel Cup races held at the Talladega Superspeedway in 2005.

BATHURST (MOUNT PANORAMA CIRCUIT), AUSTRALIA

The Australian Tourist Trophy for motorcycles was the first race run on the Mount Panorama circuit in 1938, in front of 20,000 enthusiastic spectators. The 3.8-mile (6.2-km) -long circuit forms a formidable opponent for drivers, with hairpin bends, sharp climbs, and the long, downhill Conrod Straight. While it has been used for many categories of racing in the past, the circuit is best known for the Bathurst 1,000 event for touring cars. This race began as a 500-mile (805km) event in 1963, changing to a 620-mile (1,000km) race ten years later. Bathurst legend Peter Brock first won the event in 1972 and went on to claim a total of nine wins in 30 starts. Mount Panorama is classified as a road circuit and is open to regular traffic apart from on race days.

TARGA FLORIO, ITALY

Once memorably described as "not so much a race as an ordeal," the Targa Florio was first organized by car enthusiast Count Vincenzo Florio in 1906. In its early days, racers and their onboard mechanic not only had to contend with extreme hairpin bends, treacherous mountain conditions, and unreliable cars, but also wolves and bandits. Yet, from the 1920s to the 1960s, this grueling event on the island of Sicily attracted the world's best drivers, with winners including Tazio Nuvolari, Achille Varzi, Stirling Moss, and Graham Hill. In 1924, car designers Ferdinand Porsche and Enzo Ferrari, as well as future legendary team boss Alfred Neubauer, all took part. Two years later, Eliska Junkova became the first woman to enter. Safety concerns mounted over the years, however, and in 1973, the race was downgraded to a minor event.

▲ V8 Supercars speed through the New South Wales countryside during the 2005 Bathurst 1,000.

▼ In the Sicilian village of Collesano, Italy, a typically enthusiastic crowd watches the 1965 Targa Florio.

▶ Georges Philippe
(the pseudonym of Baron
de Rothschild), races his
Bugatti Type 35C through
Tabac corner during the
first-ever Monaco Grand
Prix, in 1929. Behind him
is Rudolf Caracciola in
a Mercedes-Benz SSK.
Caracciola finished third.

MONACO, 1929

Sixteen cars started the first-ever Monaco Grand Prix, on April 14, 1929. 100 laps and three hours, 56 minutes, and 11 seconds later, Anglo-French driver William Grover-Williams crossed the finish line first in his Bugatti Type 35B. The race had been the brainchild of wealthy businessman Anthony Noghes. He set up the event with the patronage and support of the ruling Grimaldi family, particularly Prince Louis II, and Monaco's most famous driver, Louis Chirron. The race posed a harsh test to drivers, with its tight turns, downhill runs, and narrow raceways barricaded off from spectators by sandbags and temporary fences. "Any respectable traffic system would have covered the track with 'Danger' signposts left, right, and center," commented one journal, *La Vie Automobile*, immediately after the race. Yet the Monaco GP grew and grew, becoming one of the most star-studded and glamorous motor races in the world. Famous features of the legendary circuit include the curving tunnel, Casino Square, Tabac, the tight Loews hairpin, and the Rascasse and Sainte Devote corners.

DREAMS OF GLORY

All over the world, thousands of young people have dreams of success and glory in motorsports. A number of them have the chance to showcase their wits and skills against others in the many different levels of amateur racing. But only a few progress from there, moving up through the ranks to compete at the very highest level.

▲ *Formula One world champion Graham Hill looks on as his son Damon, a future world champion, is fitted into his own child-size car.*

LIVING THE DREAM

Some drivers and riders are inspired by a thrilling race that they watched as a child, while others will have grown up in a family that is steeped in motor racing. Motorsports dynasties have a long history—from father and son Antonio and Alberto Ascari in the early days of racing, to NASCAR's famous Petty, Allison, and Andretti clans, and Gilles and Jacques Villeneuve in Formula One. Those without family connections or wealth still race, hoping that their performances will attract major sponsors. In all cases, it takes thousands of hours of race practice, personal sacrifices, and significant financial backing for their dream to be fulfilled. Small operations that self-finance their own teams and drivers are known as "privateers." Being a privateer was once no barrier to entering and competing at the highest level. Privateers used to win F1 races fairly regularly, but the last such victory was by Jo Siffert in Rob Walker Racing's Lotus at the 1968 British

▼ *Matt Neal drives a Honda Integra for the Halfords team in the British Touring Car Championship (BTCC). In 1999, he became the first privateer in the modern era to win a BTCC race, driving a Nissan Primera.*

GP. In other classes of motorsports, privateers still compete at the top. Former WRC title holder Sebastian Loeb, for example, competed in the 2006 World Rally Championship as part of the Kronos Citroën privateer outfit.

LICENSED TO THRILL

In the amateur arena, motorsports is a booming activity for both participants and fans. Thousands of racers are happy to stay at that level, but some use it as a starting point on the long road to potential stardom. Most amateur racing is centered on local and regional clubs, which run hill climbs, trials, junior rallies, dirt races, and many other events. Rules and regulations vary, but many countries require special licenses in order to race. In the U.K., beginners start by obtaining the Motor Sport Association Non-Race Class B License, a document that comes with *The Blue Book*— a guide to the rules of motorsports. Classes and competitions exist for cars and bikes with only a small amount of equipment and vehicle alterations. For cars, the minimum requirements may consist of flameproof clothing (or an

▲ Jules Bianchi of France leads the pack during a Junior Karting Championship race in Braga, Portugal, in August 2004.

▼ In 2004, 13-year-old John Edwards won the Red Bull Driver Search—a competition to find a future U.S. F1 champion. Edwards had competed in karting and open-wheel racing for a number of years.

approved riding suit for bikes), a crash helmet, a fire extinguisher, and a timing strut that allows lap times to be recorded. Many forms of amateur racing require further safety equipment such as competition seats, racing harnesses, and approved tires and roll cages.

MOVING ON UP

Promising young racers need to gain as much race and technical experience as possible. This includes not only riding or driving as often as they can, but also attending race days at higher levels. There, they can gain experience of what goes on behind the scenes in the pits and are also able to discuss race tactics and techniques with more experienced racers. In many countries, racing schools have been established that offer everything from half-day race experience sessions for genuine beginners to intensive racecraft training courses for those wishing to move up one or more levels. In more recent years, competitions and racing classes have been set up specifically to seek out the best young talent, which can be nurtured and placed with

teams racing at higher levels of competition. For example, A. J. Allmendinger's excellent performances in the 2000 Champ Car Stars of Tomorrow karting competition earned him a racing scholarship, drives in the Barber Dodge Pro Series, and then a move into Formula Atlantic. He then entered Champ Cars in 2004.

As well as offering exciting, low-cost racing for thousands of people, karting has a history of being a fertile breeding ground for some of motorsports' great racers. Michael Schumacher, Ayrton Senna, Juan Pablo Montoya, Jeff Gordon, and Helio Castroneves all began their careers in karting, which has been especially strong in Europe and South America. In addition, each winner of the Indianapolis 500 between 2000 and 2004 had a karting background with championship wins in South America.

MANAGING A RACE TEAM

A major race team is a highly sophisticated, complex, and expensive operation. Managing a successful outfit demands a great range of attributes, from tough negotiating skills to cunning race strategies.

▲ Team trucks line up in the paddock at the Texas Motor Speedway for a 1999 NASCAR Winston Cup race.

▼ The Ferrari transporter arrives at the 1960 Dutch GP, laden with the team's Dino 246 cars.

▲ Tom Kristensen poses at the launch of the diesel-powered Audi R10 sports car (designed for endurance racing) in Paris, France, in December 2005.

▼ Formula One cars their and components tend to be the most expensive in motorsports, as shown by these approximate costs for Jaguar's 2004 car, the R5.

AN EXPENSIVE BUSINESS

Motor racing costs a lot of money, and the higher the level of competition, the more expensive it gets. In Formula One, the top teams can spend almost $50 million per season on testing alone. Many millions more go into the development and construction of vehicles, the purchase of equipment and parts, and the salaries of a support staff that is often measured in the hundreds. Richard Childress Racing, one of the most successful NASCAR outfits, employs around 280 staff. In 2006, McLaren's total workforce was reported to be 524, while Williams' was 513. The logistics of moving a large, sophisticated race team and its large quantities of equipment around the world are complex and expensive. In Formula One, teams travel almost 100,000 miles (160,000km) each year for testing and races. They will haul as much as 300 tons of equipment from race to race, of which the two racing cars only make up 1.5 tons. Airfares and accommodation are additional costs, alongside salaries in excess of $20 million per year for the best racers.

TEAM BOSSES

Teams vary in size from small privateers to the works or factory teams that are financed and technically supported by major vehicle manufacturers. The biggest of these, such as Ferrari and Toyota, have budgets in excess of $400 million per season. Other major race operations may not be works teams, but they benefit from having a leading engine supplier as a partner such as McLaren and its F1 engine supplier, Mercedes. Whatever its size, at the head

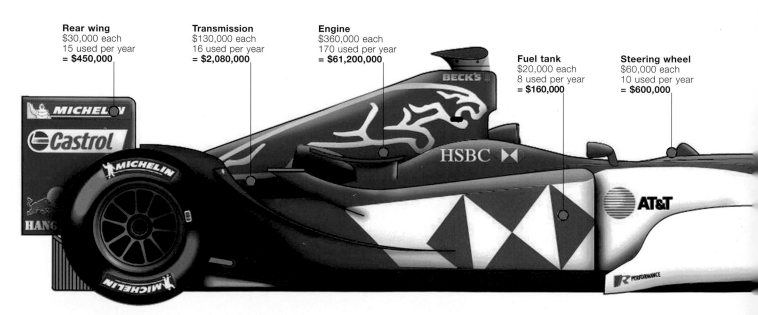

Rear wing
$30,000 each
15 used per year
= **$450,000**

Transmission
$130,000 each
16 used per year
= **$2,080,000**

Engine
$360,000 each
170 used per year
= **$61,200,000**

Fuel tank
$20,000 each
8 used per year
= **$160,000**

Steering wheel
$60,000 each
10 used per year
= **$600,000**

of a successful race team is a highly experienced team boss, or principal. Some bosses, such as Indy racing's Bobby Rahal of the Rahal-Letterman team, were drivers themselves. Others started on the engineering side. McLaren's Ron Dennis, for example, was a mechanic for Jochen Rindt's Formula One car. Race weekends are very busy times for team bosses, as they oversee team strategy and are frequently at the center of media attention. Away from races, they are heavily involved in complex negotiations with sponsors, drivers, suppliers of parts and equipment, and the sport's authorities.

TEAM CHANGES

The high costs of entering top-class racing come with absolutely no guarantee of a place on the podium. As a result, many teams find themselves under pressure, losing sponsors and being forced to withdraw from competitions. In recent years, many teams in Formula One, such as Minardi and Jordan, have left the scene, while the successful CART team Patrick Racing, which moved to the Indy Racing League in 2004, was unable to obtain a sponsor in 2005 and folded.

▲ Flavio Briatore was the team boss of Benetton before becoming the principal of Renault in 2000.

▲ Eddie Jordan (right), talking to F1 boss Bernie Ecclestone, was the team owner of Jordan before its sale to Midland in 2005.

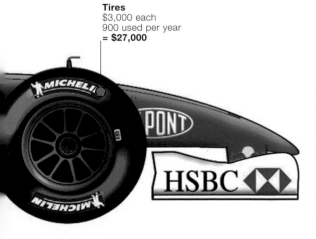

Tires
$3,000 each
900 used per year
= **$27,000**

◄ Cars and equipment owned by the now defunct Minardi Formula One team are ready for auction in 2004. Minardi entered F1 in 1985; twenty years later, the team was sold to Red Bull Racing

Team changes also occur when manufacturers withdraw or drop out for one or more seasons. In rallying, Citroën sat out 2006, and Mitsubishi's Ralliart team missed the 2006 and 2007 seasons. Entering a new team in the F1 World Championship requires a $50 million bond, a type of payment that is made up front to the FIA, which is then repaid once the team begins to compete. A way around this is to buy an existing team. Examples include Benetton's purchase of Toleman F1 in the mid-1980s and Honda's acquisition of the BAR team in 2005.

CUTTING COSTS

In recent years, some classes of particularly expensive motorsports, including MotoGP, the WRC, and Formula One, have made rule changes in an attempt to cut costs and attract more entrants. With tobacco sponsors leaving the sport, this is becoming even more important. The World Rally Championship, for example, has altered its racing calendar to cut down on travel by introducing paired rallies—two events held one weekend after another in which the same engine and chassis must be used. In 2005, MotoGP's rules were changed to only allow one qualifying session, while in Formula One, proposed cost-cutting measures for 2008 and beyond include engines that must be used for three races, no more than two changes to a car's bodywork per season, and the use of cheaper, less advanced transmissions and control units.

▼ Petter Solberg and his codriver, Philip Mills (at the rear), celebrate victory with the whole Subaru team after the 2004 Rally of Italy.

MOTORSPORTS AND THE MEDIA

Media interest, especially in the form of live television coverage, is absolutely vital to motorsports. The live televising of NASCAR since the 1970s, for example, was credited with sparking a huge increase in public interest, helping turn it from a regional to a national phenomenon.

MEDIA POWER— MOTORSPORTS BENEFIT

Coverage on television and the Internet has allowed major races to be viewed by millions of people who are unable to attend the events themselves. It is also the way that the emerging markets for motorsports are being developed in China, India, Russia, Malaysia, and other populous countries in eastern Europe and the Far East. Possibly most important of all, it is the TV broadcasts and extensive media interest in motorsports that attracts investment from sponsors and advertisers. The success of motorsports is heavily dependent on the financial support of these organizations, who pay a large proportion of the often substantial costs of modern, professional racing.

SPONSORSHIP

In the early 1960s, NASCAR driver Fred Lorenzen was one of the first to put together a sponsorship package. A North Carolina car dealer paid him $6,000 for an entire 29-race season—just over $200 per race. In 2000, UPS sponsored Dale Jarrett's NASCAR to the tune of around $400,000 per race. The main or primary sponsors of a major NASCAR race team can pay $10–20 million per season, while in Formula One, the figure can rise up to $60 million. For this, a primary sponsor will have access to the team and drivers, their brand name and logos will be displayed in prominent positions on the car, and the cars and clothing

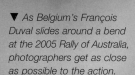
▼ As Belgium's François Duval slides around a bend at the 2005 Rally of Australia, photographers get as close as possible to the action.

◄ *In 2005, Elliott Sadler's Ford colorfully displays the branding of M&Ms, the NASCAR team's primary sponsor.*

►► *Modern television coverage offers viewers dramatic driver's-eye viewpoints, taking them to the heart of the action.*

may be in the brand's colors. Sometimes the brand or company name becomes part of the team name—Red Bull Skoda in rallying and Marlboro-McLaren in F1 during the 1980s, for example. In addition to primary sponsors, there are lower levels of sponsorship such as cosponsors and trade linkups. These companies pay less, receive less prominent space on the car (on the side fins and side mirrors, for example), but they seek to benefit from media exposure, hospitality, and being associated with a successful team.

TOBACCO SPONSORSHIP

From Gold Leaf, F1's first car sponsor, to R. J. Reynolds, the sponsor of NASCAR's Winston Cup for more than thirty years, tobacco companies, such as West, Marlboro, British American, and Seita (the owners of the Gauloises and Gitanes brands), have pumped hundreds of millions of dollars into motorsports. In recent years, this has caused increasing controversy as antitobacco advertising laws have been applied. The 2005 Hungarian F1 GP was the last to occur before the European Union (EU) ban on tobacco advertising in motorsports came into force, but it is still unclear how events held outside of the EU, but still televised within it, will fare.

▲ *In 2005, the Red Bull Formula One team's association with the launch of a new Star Wars movie was typical of the high-profile sponsorship and marketing deals that F1 attracts.*

MERCHANDISING MOTORSPORTS

Away from sponsorship, teams obtain smaller, yet still crucial, amounts of income from areas such as television rights, race winnings, and the merchandising of official team programs, clothing, and collectibles. Racing souvenirs range from driver figurines to race programs, while auctions sell all types of memorabilia, from a driver's racewear (Ayrton Senna's Rheos helmet sold for around $75,000 in 1998) to entire vintage cars. In September 2004, a Bonhams auction for a Mercedes 38/250 SSK—the type of car that won the 1927 German GP—fetched more than $8 million.

IN THE KNOW

Broadcasting modern motor racing is a highly sophisticated operation. It is no longer a matter of simply pointing cameras at the action; viewers now demand background details on the teams, drivers, and circuits, as well as up-to-the-minute data on race standings and strategies. On the track, lightweight cameras offer stunning shots of the race from the driver's or rider's viewpoint. Pit lane and paddock reporters interview the teams and drivers, while cameras show the race vehicles close up. Many motorsports commentators have an extensive background in racing. Ex-racers often work as analysts and commentators. NASCAR's Rusty Wallace was racing in 2005 but was a TV analyst the next season, while in F1, world champion James Hunt formed a memorable on-air partnership for more than ten years with veteran broadcaster Murray Walker.

GEARHEADS

Devoted fans of motorsports are nicknamed "gearheads" in the U.S. They follow their favorite classes of racing through the Internet, magazines, television, and radio. And every year, despite the great expense of attending many major events, millions of fans flock to tracks, rally courses, and arenas on race days.

HUGE NUMBERS

Unlike sports events that take place in compact stadiums, it can be hard to gauge the number of fans at large motorsports venues. What is known is that attendances are huge. Formula One regularly attracts almost 300,000 spectators over the three days of practice, qualifying, and racing. In 2004, the World Rally Championship's 16 races were attended by more than ten million

▲ *Two female members of Ferrari's tifosi wear red clothing, wigs, and face paint to show their loyalty to the legendary Italian team.*

fans, while historic meetings such as the Goodwood Revival in the U.K. may attract 100,000 spectators over the weekend. The Indianapolis Motor Speedway is believed to hold the most race fans of all. Estimates have varied over the years, but a 2003 study found that the arena contained 257,325 permanent seats.

LOYALTY AND DEVOTION

Some fans are drawn to their local events regardless of who is racing. In 1987, for example, the first Formula One Grand Prix (F1 GP) in Japan for ten years saw a staggering two million people apply for the 100,000 tickets. Other fans follow and support a certain driver, team, or manufacturer. Among the most devoted are Ferrari's *tifosi*, who follow the fortunes of the team in Formula One, sports, and GT racing.

THE RACE-DAY EXPERIENCE

The sights and sounds of race day are truly intoxicating to a gearhead. At larger open-wheel, stock car, and motorcycle racing events, visitors may show up days in advance, camping or parking close to the track and holding parties and events of their own. There is usually plenty to see and do around a major race circuit. Some autograph hunters, eager to meet their heroes, line up at the paddock entrance for long periods or try to obtain a highly sought-after paddock pass that will give them access to the garages, the teams, and the drivers or riders. Spectators often have a variety of ways to keep up with the racing action—from the giant scoring towers that are used at many NASCAR and Champ Car circuits to on-course radio broadcasts. Fans may even rent radio scanners with which they can hear teams and drivers communicating with each other. Some tracks offer better views than others. Malaysia's Sepang International Circuit, for example, was built in a valley so that fans can see 90 percent of the entire track from some vantage points.

▲ *Italian motorcycling star Valentino Rossi is mobbed by fans after winning the Czech MotoGP at Brno in 2003. Rossi went on to win the World Championship, to the delight of his many supporters.*

◄◄ *A sell-out crowd at the 150,061-capacity Texas Motor Speedway watches the 2005 O'Reilly 300—a Busch Series NASCAR race. Kasey Kahne surged to a thrilling victory from 25th place on the starting grid.*

▲ *A visitor to the European GP in 1999 tries out a roll cage simulator at the Mercedes stand. Displays, exhibits, and interactive games and simulations are part of the race weekend fun that is provided for race fans at many major motorsports events.*

RULES AND CONTROVERSY

Ever since 1895, when Emile Levassor crossed the finish line in what is regarded as the first true race (run from Paris to Bordeaux in France), motorsports and controversy have gone hand in hand. Levassor was disqualified because his car was not the required four-seater vehicle. From that point on, the sport has seen many more disqualifications, controversies, and debates over rules and tactics.

▲ *Jenson Button's BAR-Honda 007 is checked before the 2005 San Marino GP.*

SCRUTINEERS AND INSPECTION

Most classes of motorsports have precise, lengthy, and complex sets of rules regarding the construction and preparation of race vehicles and equipment. Teams of vehicle inspectors, or scrutineers, are employed in many classes in order to carefully examine a vehicle in great detail. They check that it complies with all of the sport's safety regulations and measure the exact dimensions and positions of key parts of the machine. Immediately after races in many classes, the car and the driver are weighed on a device

called a weigh bridge, and the scrutineers again take key measurements. Samples of fuel and even tires may be taken to be analyzed in labs. Any major problems or irregularities may lead to disqualification and the loss of points. At Monza, in the 2004 World Superbike Championship, Chris Vermeulen was disqualified and lost the points for his second-place finish after it was found that the tilt switch on his bike (to cut the engine if the bike falls on its side) was not working. At the 2005 San Marino GP, BAR cars driven by Jenson Button and Takuma Sato were found to be underweight, due to a hidden second fuel tank that kept them above the 1,320-lb. (600kg) minimum at the post-race weigh-in. The team received a two-race ban. The reality of motorsports' many and complex rules mean that teams will protest or appeal against many decisions, sometimes with success. For example, in 1998, motorcyclist Kazuto Sakata was disqualified from the Australian GP after tests appeared to show that he was using leaded fuel that was banned that season. On appeal, Sakata won, and the reinstated points gave him the 125cc World Championship.

▲ *NASCAR inspectors use one of a series of official templates to check the shape of this Toyota Craftsman truck.*

BENDING OR BREAKING?

Most race teams are on the lookout for loopholes in the rules or ways to stretch them as far as possible to gain the advantage. Rule bending and breaking was constant in the earlier years of NASCAR. In 1964, for example, team owner Bud Moore's car was ruled to be sitting too low. While Moore argued with an official, one of his mechanics secretly slid several rocks underneath the front tires and rolled the car forward. The car

passed when it was remeasured! Sometimes, the interpretation of rules causes controversy. In the 1970s, as ground effect (see p. 129) was investigated, Brabham produced a novel car, the BT46B, which used a giant fan at the back. The fan sucked away the air from underneath the car, helping it "stick" to the road and giving Niki Lauda one of his easiest Grand Prix wins. Movable aerodynamic devices were not permitted, but the Brabham team argued that the fan's main purpose was to cool down the engine. Its arguments fell on deaf ears as the car was banned, although, controversially, Lauda's win and points were allowed to stand. The owner of Brabham at the time was Bernie Ecclestone, who is now a powerful figure in the Formula One authorities.

CONTROVERSIAL TACTICS

Drivers and riders must abide by official rules and mutual agreements. There are accepted ways of racing, and those who step over the line may be disqualified. At the 2003 MotoGP race in Japan, for example, Makato Tamada barged past Spain's Sete Gibernau and was later disqualified for what was considered to be "riding in an irresponsible manner." Unfair or dangerous tactics can also spark confrontation. For example, Tony Stewart's bumping of Kasey Kahne at NASCAR's 2004 Tropicana 400 prompted an argument and brawl between the two men's pit crews. Controversy also often surrounds the giving of team orders such as when a lower-placed driver in a championship is instructed to let his or her better-placed teammate pass. On the last lap of the final race in the 1977 AMA 125cc Motocross Championship, Bob Hannah was given the pit-lane instruction to let his 17-year-old teammate Broc Glover through so that he could win the title. In 1998, David Coulthard let Mika Hakkinen pass him to win the Australian Formula One Grand Prix after a prerace agreement. This infuriated fans and the authorities because it did not come at the climax of the season but in the very first race. The FIA then banned team orders at such a stage in the season.

◄◄ The controversial Brabham BT46B "fan car" on show during the U.K.'s Goodwood Festival of Speed in June 2004.

▲ Japan's Makato Tamada (6) attempts to pass Sete Gibernau of Spain during the Pacific GP in 2003. The Japanese rider was later disqualified.

◄◄ Race officials try to break up the pit-lane brawl between the NASCAR teams of Tony Stewart and Kasey Kahne in 2004.

◄ Michael Schumacher is furious with BAR driver Takuma Sato after a collision at the 2005 Belgian GP.

▲ A Renault pit crewman checks the pressure of the team's Michelin tires before the qualifying session.

▲▲ U.S. race fans show their anger at the end of the race. Michelin later refunded the price of their tickets.

▼ Michael Schumacher approaches the famous "yard of bricks" at Indianapolis.

THE U.S. GP, 2005

After a series of failures during practice and qualifying, tire manufacturer Michelin declared that its tires were unsafe for the Formula One U.S. GP at Indianapolis on June 19, 2005. Proposals to save the race included limiting the speed of Michelin-tired cars at the high-speed, banked turn 13, fitting a chicane to the turn, and running a nonchampionship event. In the end, the race went ahead, but after the parade lap, the 14 cars with Michelin tires retired into the pits. Amid boos and jeers from the crowd, the remaining six cars lined up on the grid to race. Michael Schumacher and Rubens Barrichello claimed a one-two for Ferrari, while Jordan's Narain Karthikeyan became the first Indian driver to win World Championship points. But his achievement could not mask the fact that thousands of fans at the circuit and millions more television viewers had been cheated out of a real race.

▲ Six cars line up in their qualifying positions on an almost empty starting grid at the 2005 U.S. GP. The two red cars of Ferrari qualified in fifth and seventh, the yellow Jordans in 17th and 19th, and the two Minardi cars in 18th and 20th. All six cars were running on Bridgestone tires.

RACING LEGENDS

▲ *Fernando Alonso's win at the Chinese GP in Shanghai in October 2005 won the F1 constructor's championship for Renault.*

Throughout its history, motor racing has witnessed extraordinary feats of daring, courage, and skill exhibited by its greatest competitors. Here are a selection of some of the best motorsports drivers and riders.

FERNANDO ALONSO
SPAIN, BORN 1981

In 2001, Fernando Alonso became Formula One's third-youngest driver, racing impressively in the underpowered Minardi. After one year as a Renault test driver, he began racing for them in 2003. In his second race for the team, in Malaysia, Alonso became the youngest F1 driver to claim a pole position. An epic struggle followed with Michael Schumacher for the lead at the Spanish GP, where he proved his star status to his compatriots. Alonso then started and finished the Hungarian GP in first place, becoming the sport's youngest winner at 22 years, 26 days. In 2005, with seven wins and five second places in 19 races, he took the title ahead of Kimi Räikkönen and was hailed as the natural successor to Michael Schumacher.

GRAHAM HILL
U.K., 1929–1975

Norman Graham Hill's highly successful Formula One career—14 race wins, two world titles, and three championship second places—often overshadows the fact that he was a true all-arounder. He is the only driver to have won motor racing's "triple crown" of the Indy 500 (1966), the Formula One World Championship (1962, 1968), and the Le Mans 24 Hours (1972). He also won the Tourist Trophy (TT) in 1963 and 1964. Hill made his Grand Prix debut at Monaco in 1958 and went on to win that race five times. It was also the location of his final Grand Prix in July 1975. Tragically, in November 1975, Hill and five members of his race team were killed in a plane crash. When his son Damon took the F1 World Championship in 1996, they became the only father and son to have won the competition.

▲ *Despite not passing his driving test until he was 24, the charismatic Graham Hill went on to become one of motor racing's true legends.*

▶▶ *Ari Vatanen races through the snow in his Peugeot 205, on the way to victory at the 1985 Rally of Sweden. In 1999, the Finn became a Member of the European Parliament (MEP).*

MALCOLM SMITH
U.S., BORN 1941

The son of a gold miner turned sheep farmer, Malcolm Smith got his first real dirt bike at the age of 15. After some success in local races, his big break came when Edison Dye, an importer of Swedish Husqvarna motorcycles, asked Smith to ride for him. Smith and Husqvarna dominated the sport as he enjoyed huge success in off-road competitions. He won the legendary Baja 1,000 race a record six times, the Baja 500 four times, and was an eight-time gold medalist at the International Six Day Trials between 1966 and 1976. His appearance in the influential 1972 film, *On Any Sunday*, helped popularize off-road racing. A successful businessman who sold motorcycle racing equipment, Smith was inducted into the Motorcycle Hall of Fame in 1998.

ARI VATANEN
FINLAND, BORN 1952

Ari Vatanen's first major title was the 1976 British Rally Championship. He won the title again in 1980, the year that he won his first World Rally Championship event—the demanding Acropolis Rally. The Acropolis was one of three wins in 1981 that propelled Vatanen to the WRC crown. A horrific, life-threatening 124mph (200km/h) crash during the Rally of Argentina in 1985 took almost two years to recover from. Vatanen moved into rally-raids with Peugeot, winning the Dakar Rally three times (1987 and 1989–1990). A fourth win came in 1991 when he was driving for Citroën. Other rally-raid successes included the Hong Kong–Beijing in 1993 and 1996, the Baja–Spain in 1996, and the U.A.E. Desert Challenge in 1997.

RICHARD PETTY

U.S., BORN 1937

The most successful driver in NASCAR history, with 200 race wins, 127 pole positions, seven Daytona 500 titles, and a record of seven Grand National or Winston Cups, Petty is a living legend. Part of a major racing dynasty that includes his father, Lee, his son, Kyle, and his grandson, Adam (who died in a crash in 2000), Petty joined NASCAR in 1958 at the age of 21. The following season, he was Rookie of the Year, with an impressive nine top-ten finishes. Petty finished in the top five of a race an astonishing 550 times, with his first win coming at Charlotte Speedway in 1960 and his last, 24 years later, at Daytona.

Petty was instrumental in the rise of NASCAR. A nine-time winner of the Most Popular Driver award, he is an icon in the U.S., where he is known as "the King." Since retiring in 1992, Petty has run a successful NASCAR team of his own.

IVAN MAUGER

NEW ZEALAND, BORN 1939

Mauger's 30-year-long career in speedway was ignited in 1966 at the World Championship in Sweden, in which he finished fourth but won two of the races. In 14 years of the World Speedway individual competition between 1966 and 1979, he finished outside the top four only once, winning the competition six times. He also won four World Team titles, two World Pairs titles, and three individual Long Track crowns. From 1969 to 1982, he was the official factory rider for Czech manufacturer Jawa, and his battles with a series of highly talented Scandinavian speedway riders, most notably Denmark's Ole Olsen, attracted hordes of new speedway fans.

▲ Ivan Mauger, shown here riding a 500cc Jawa in his home country of New Zealand in 2003.

▼ Richard Petty, in his famous car number 43, battles for the lead with Bobby Allison (28) and Harry Gant (33) at the 1981 Champion Spark Plug 400.

DALE EARNHARDT
U.S., 1951–2001

Earnhardt entered NASCAR in 1975, recording more than 70 race wins in the top-class Winston Cup and claiming his first championship in 1980. Six more titles followed (1986–1987, 1990–1991, 1993–1994) as he earned a reputation as a relentless and determined driver, nicknamed "the Intimidator." Earnhardt built a family racing dynasty, setting up a multimillion dollar race company, while his two sons, Dale, Jr. and Kenny, race successfully. Considering his talent, it was extraordinary that he failed to win the Daytona 500 until 1998, on his 20th attempt. At the same event three years later, the much-loved American died after a crash in his last lap (see pp. 14–15).

▲ *Dale Earnhardt pushes his Chevrolet to the limit at the Pennzoil 400 race, held at the Homestead-Miami Speedway in 2000.*

▼ *Mike Hailwood prepares for the green light in 1964.*

MIKE HAILWOOD
U.K., 1941–1981

A true all-arounder, the charismatic Hailwood was one of the finest motorcyclists of all time, winning nine world titles and 76 Grand Prix during the 1960s. Having done it all on two wheels, Hailwood switched to four. He showed his speed in more than 50 F1 races, but he never quite matched his earlier success. He did, however, win the 1972 Formula Two European title and was third at the 1969 Le Mans 24 Hours. Hailwood was in fourth in the 1974 Formula One World Championship when an accident curtailed his F1 career. In 1978, after 11 years away from bikes, Hailwood made a sensational comeback, winning the Isle of Man TT and claiming his tenth motorcycling world title.

PEDRO RODRIGUEZ
MEXICO, 1940–1971

Pedro Rodriguez was only 20 when he and his even younger brother, Ricardo, were runners-up at Le Mans in 1960. Ricardo was hired by the Ferrari F1 team but tragically died in a crash in 1962. Pedro raced in 55 Grand Prix, winning twice, but he had more success in endurance racing. He won the Le Mans 24 Hours in 1968 and the Daytona 24 Hours twice (1970–1971). Rodriguez was at the peak of his powers when he entered a minor sports car race in Germany. While battling for the lead, a slower car forced Rodriguez into the wall, his car bursting into flames. The Mexican died shortly afterward.

SEBASTIAN LOEB
FRANCE, BORN 1974

Sebastian Loeb's childhood dream was to be a gymnast or an acrobat, but instead he turned to rallying, winning the Junior World Rally Championship in 2001. Loeb's first full WRC season—with Citroën in 2002—saw him win his debut event, the Rally of Germany. One year later, Loeb won three races and pushed Petter Solberg to the very limit, losing the championship by just one point. In 2004, Loeb bounced back, winning the world title and becoming the first nonScandinavian to win the Rally of Sweden. Citroën announced that it was pulling out of the WRC after 2005, but Loeb made the most of his last season with the team, becoming the first driver to win six rallies in a row. At the Rally of Japan, in October, he sealed his second WRC title with three races to go.

▶ *Sebastian Loeb surges through water in his Citroën Xsara, on the way to victory at the 2004 Rally of Australia. It was his sixth win of the season.*

◀ *Riding a Yamaha YZR-M1, Valentino Rossi powers to pole position for the 2005 British GP at Donington Park. Early in 2006, Rossi tested a Formula One Ferrari, fueling rumors of a move onto four wheels.*

VALENTINO ROSSI
ITALY, BORN 1979

Rossi displayed his very special talent by winning the 125cc world crown in 1997 and, two years later, the 250cc title, both with Aprilia. Moving to Honda, he won the GP500 crown in 2001. With the arrival of powerful 989cc bikes for the first MotoGP season, most riders took time to adapt, but not Rossi, who won eight of the first nine races on the way to the 2002 title—a feat that he repeated the following year. Lightning-quick and fearless, the Italian stunned the MotoGP world by switching to Yamaha for 2004. The team had not won a title since 1992, but Rossi swept all before him, winning nine races and the world crown. It was business as usual in 2005, as he clinched the title with four races left.

DANICA SUE PATRICK
U.S., BORN 1982

As a teenager, Patrick was a karting star, winning an incredible 39 out of 49 races in 1996. In 2002, racing for the Rahal team, she became the first woman to record a podium finish in the Toyota Atlantic Championship. A series of solid drives in 2004 saw her finish third overall, and the following year, Rahal-Letterman Racing chose her to drive for its IndyCar team. Patrick triumphed again at the 2005 Indianapolis 500, where she set the fastest practice speed (229.33mph, or 369.88km/h) and led the race, the first woman to do so (see pp. 118–119). At only 23 years of age, she won her first pole position in July 2005, at Kansas Speedway.

▲ *Danica Sue Patrick at the 2005 Indy 500, where she finished fourth—the highest placing by a female driver in the race's history.*

►► *Driving for McLaren, Niki Lauda won five races in 1984. He took the title by just half a point from Alain Prost—the closest margin in F1 history.*

▲ *Bobby Rahal in 1992, the year he became the last owner-driver to win the CART Championship.*

▼ *Spanish rally driver Carlos Sainz greets his fans during a tribute for his retirement in Madrid, Spain, on November 28, 2004.*

BOBBY RAHAL

U.S., BORN 1953

One of the greatest drivers in CART (now Champ Car) racing, Rahal won 24 races and three championships, in 1986, 1987, and 1992. He began racing in Sports Car Club of America (SCCA) competitions in the early 1970s. After pursuing a degree in history, Rahal joined Formula Atlantic, where he finished second to Gilles Villeneuve in 1977. As well as racing in Formula One and Two in Europe, Rahal also enjoyed success in sports car racing, winning the Daytona 24 Hours in 1981 and the 12 Hours of Sebring in 1987. He retired from driving in 1998, and has since been the boss of Jaguar racing and has also headed his own race team.

JEAN-PIERRE WIMILLE

FRANCE, 1906–1949

Wimille began racing in Bugatti cars, switched to Alfa Romeos, and then returned to Bugatti as a works driver. He won the 1937 Le Mans 24 Hours and repeated the feat two years later. During World War II, Wimille was a member of the French resistance and was considered a national hero. In 1947 and 1948, driving Alfa Romeo Tipo 158s, he won numerous races, including the Belgian, Swiss, French, and Italian Grand Prix. Wimille wore a crash helmet for the first time during a practice for a race in Argentina in 1949, but he was tragically killed in a crash.

CARLOS SAINZ

SPAIN, BORN 1962

Sainz made his rallying debut in a SEAT Panda in 1980, and seven years later, he entered his first WRC rally, the Rally of Portugal. Racing for Toyota, 1990 was a landmark year, as he won a WRC race for the first time (the Acropolis Rally) and then won the entire championship. He took the title again in 1992, also for Toyota. In 2004, Sainz set a new record when he won his 26th WRC rally (in Argentina), passing Colin McRae's 25 wins. He formally retired at the end of that year, but he did make two more WRC appearances for Citroën in 2005. In addition, he finished 11th for Volkswagen in the 2006 Dakar Rally.

NIKI LAUDA

AUSTRIA, BORN 1949

Starting off in hill climbing, Lauda ran up large debts in his early racing career before securing an F1 drive with Ferrari in 1974. The following year, he won five races on his way to the World Championship. In 1976, he suffered a horrific crash at the German GP, falling into a coma with terrible burns to his head. Lauda then staged one of sports' greatest-ever comebacks. Returning just six weeks later, he finished fourth in the Italian GP and only lost the world title by one point when he considered conditions at the last race of the season to be too dangerous to enter. He then won the 1977 World Championship with two races to go, before walking out on Ferrari to join Brabham. He retired in 1979 but returned with McLaren in 1982, winning his third World Championship in 1984.

JUAN MANUEL FANGIO
ARGENTINA, 1911–1995

A masterful racer, Fangio developed his incredible driving reactions, stamina, and tactical skills on epic Argentinian races such as the tough, 6,200-mile (10,000-km) -long Gran Premio del Norte, which he won in 1940. After World War II and at the age of 38, he was sponsored by the Argentinian Government to race in Europe. In 1950, driving an Alfa Romeo, Fangio battled with Giuseppe Farina, losing the world title by just three points. He made up for it the following year, winning the first and last Grand Prix and beating Alberto Ascari to the title. Fangio missed a lot of the 1952 season after breaking his neck in an accident, but he returned to be the runner-up in 1953. Between 1954 and 1957, Fangio drove for Mercedes-Benz, Ferrari, and Maserati. It did not matter which car he was in as he swept away the competition and won four World Championships in a row. At the 1957 German GP, Fangio broke his own lap record six times during the race. The following year, he retired from racing after the French GP, getting out of his car and saying to a mechanic, "It is finished." In an age of many great drivers, Fangio's victory rate of 24 wins and ten second places in 51 Grand Prix is a testament to the maestro's driving prowess.

GIACOMO AGOSTINI
ITALY, BORN 1942

The most successful motorcycle rider in history, Agostini began racing in the early 1960s. After joining MV Agusta in 1965, Agostini became virtually unbeatable. His Tourist Trophy (TT) racing record illustrates this, with 13 podium finishes from 16 races, including a staggering ten wins. He also won seven straight 350cc World Championships (1968–1974) and eight 500cc crowns (1966–1972 and 1975). In total, he won 122 Grand Prix races before retiring in 1977. After a short period in car racing, he returned to bikes as Yamaha team boss, passing on his experience to the likes of Kenny Roberts, Freddie Spencer, and Eddie Lawson.

▼ *Giacomo Agostini rides an MV Agusta bike at Assen, the Dutch circuit where he recorded 14 Grand Prix victories in the 350cc and 500cc classes.*

◄ *Juan Manuel Fangio competes in the Italian GP in Monza on September 8, 1957. He finished second in his Maserati 250F.*

WAYNE RAINEY
U.S., BORN 1960

Rainey came to prominence racing on dirt tracks in California during his teens. Winning the AMA Superbike Championship in 1983, he debuted in Grand Prix racing for Yamaha in 1984 in the 250cc class. He then replaced Randy Mamola in the 500cc class in 1988. After a third-place finish in his first season and a runner-up place in 1989, he claimed the world title in 1990. Rainey repeated the feat in 1991 and 1992 but then, with a sizable lead over his rivals in 1993, a terrible crash at the Italian GP left him paralyzed. Rainey fought back, becoming a team boss for Yamaha for a while and also racing on four wheels in a specially modified superkart.

▲ *Working for the Yamaha team, Wayne Rainey drives a quad bike, or ATV, during the 1995 German GP Prix at the Nürburgring Circuit.*

ALBERTO ASCARI
ITALY, 1918–1955

Ascari's father was a former racing teammate of Enzo Ferrari, who ensured a drive for Alberto in the 1940 Mille Miglia race. After World War II, Ascari was signed on by Ferrari as the Formula One World Championship began. During the 1952 season, Ascari began an incredible run of nine consecutive Grand Prix victories that took him to the 1952 and 1953 World Championship titles. At the 1955 Monaco GP, Ascari faced a corner that he could not take and chose what he considered to be the safest way out, launching his car through the straw barriers and into Monaco harbor. He emerged with a broken nose, but no other injuries. Tragically, four days later Ascari was killed in an accident while he was testing a friend's sports car.

▼ *Alberto Ascari guides his Ferrari 500 to victory at the 1953 British GP at Silverstone.*

HIROSHI MASUOKA
JAPAN, BORN 1960

Masuoka began his motorsports career in 1979 as a road racer in Japan. After coming in third in 1985 and second in 1986 at the Australian Safari, he tackled the Dakar Rally for the first time in 1987. The 1990 race saw him surprise many observers by winning the T2 class for production vehicles. He was one of the most consistent performers in the 1990s, but victory in the Dakar Rally did not come until 2002, with codriver Pascal Maimon, and again in 2003, with Andreas Schulz. Masuoka also won the Baja Italy in 2003.

▲ *Hiroshi Masuoka plows through a steep sand dune during the 16th stage of the 22nd Dakar Rally in January 2000.*

RICK MEARS

U.S., BORN 1951

By the time he had retired in 1992, Rick "The Rocketman" Mears' place as a legend of IndyCar racing was assured. After winning Formula Vee and Super Vee titles in 1976, he secured a drive at Penske Racing as an understudy to the great Mario Andretti. Along with Al Unser, Sr. and A. J. Foyt, Mears became the third (and youngest) four-time winner of the Indy 500 (1979, 1984, 1988, and 1991). The winner of three CART Championships in 1979, 1981, and 1982, Mears' precise driving style saw him capture 40 pole positions during his career, including a record six at the Indy 500. He retired in 1992.

CALE YARBOROUGH

U.S., BORN 1939

William Caleb Yarborough began racing in 1957 and became a favorite of NASCAR fans, winning his first of four Daytona 500s in 1968 with the Wood Brothers team. Yarborough's best years came when he worked with team boss Junior Johnson— one of the few men in NASCAR as relentless and as tough as Yarborough was. His maneuvers often infuriated his rivals, and, in 1979, he was involved in a notorious brawl at the Daytona 500 with Donnie and Bobby Allison. Yarborough notched up 83 NASCAR race victories and remains the only driver to have won three Winston Cup Series Championships in a row (1976–1978). In 1984, he became the first driver to qualify for the Daytona 500 at more than 198mph (320km/h).

AYRTON SENNA

BRAZIL, 1960-1994

This mercurial Brazilian was loved by fans and feared by some drivers for his ruthless commitment to winning. Having driven karts since the age of four, Senna won the South American Kart Championship in 1977, 1978, and 1980. It was a huge jump from karts to racing in Formula Ford 1600 in Great Britain, yet Senna adjusted quickly, winning the title in 1981. He started in Formula One with Toleman in 1984 but joined Lotus the following year, winning his first F1 GP in Portugal. Impressive performances in an average car earned him a move to McLaren in 1988, the year in which he claimed his first world title with eight wins alongside teammate Alain Prost's seven. The intense rivalry between Senna and Prost (and Senna and any other driver) was a major feature of F1 in the early 1990s. Senna secured the World Championship in 1990 and 1991, and he had just started to battle with Michael Schumacher when he crashed and died at the 1994 San Marino GP (see pp. 72–73).

◀◀ *Rick Mears gives the victory salute after winning the Indy 500 in 1984.*

▼ *Ayrton Senna, seen here driving for Lotus at the 1987 Italian GP (left) and preparing for the 1991 U.S. GP (right), was diagnosed with motor coordination difficulties as a child. Yet, he went on to win 41 Grand Prix and achieve 65 pole positions.*

WALTER RÖHRL
GERMANY, BORN 1947

Röhrl was an incredibly controlled rally racer who won 14 World Rally Championship races. He became the WRC champion for the first time in 1980, but his second triumph in 1982 was even more impressive, as he was equipped with an outdated Opel Ascona and had to battle against the surging power of the four-wheel-drive Audi Quattros. His consistency meant that he finished second in 1983 and third in 1985. Röhrl was highly regarded by the teams that he raced with for his precise technical feedback and a detailed understanding of the race mechanic's art. His last season in the WRC (1987) saw him finish in 11th place, but in the same year, he won the Pikes Peak Hill Climb in record time.

DAIJIRO KATO
JAPAN, 1976–2003

Kato had the makings of a MotoGP champion. But tragically, during the first round of the 2003 World Championship, he crashed into a trackside barrier and died two weeks later from his injuries. A racing prodigy, Kato became the Japanese pocket bike champion before going on to win the Japanese Minibike Championship four times in a row (1988–1991). Kato's full-time World Championship career only began in 2000, but the following year, he was crowned the 250cc world champion, having notched up 11 Grand Prix wins during the season.

▶ Daijiro Kato in action for Honda during a free practice for the Australian GP at the Phillip Island Circuit in 2002.

TAZIO NUVOLARI
ITALY, 1892–1953

The absolutely fearless Tazio Nuvolari once won a race tied to his motorcycle, after an earlier accident had left him severely injured. He switched to cars when he was almost 40 and won all of the big races of his era—Le Mans in 1933, the Mille Miglia in 1930 and 1933, and the Targa Florio in 1931 and 1932. He notched up a total of 50 major race wins between 1927 and 1950, more than any of his rivals. Despite being seriously ill, Nuvolari raced briefly in the postwar era, his last Mille Miglia coming in 1948. More than 50,000 people attended his funeral, where he was buried in his racing colors—a yellow jersey and blue pants.

▲ Tazio Nuvolari wins the 1935 German GP, one of his greatest victories. Driving his underpowered Alfa Romeo P3 to the limit, Nuvolari defeated the mighty "Silver Arrows" of Mercedes and Auto Union on their home turf.

DEREK BELL
U.K., BORN 1941

Bell spent three years in Formula Three (1965–1967), recording seven wins in his last season, before moving up to Formula Two. Bell's time in Formula One was irregular, with only nine Grand Prix drives for a variety of teams, including Ferrari, Brabham, and Surtees. His record in sports and endurance racing was much more memorable. Bell recorded the first of an impressive five Le Mans 24 Hours victories in 1975 with codriver Jacky Ickx. To this tally, Bell added three Daytona 24 Hours wins and the 1985 and 1986 World Sports Car Championships. In 2002, and after 26 starts in the Le Mans 24 Hours, he became only the fourth driver ever to be awarded an honorary citizenship of the town of Le Mans.

JACKIE STEWART
U.K., BORN 1939

Jackie Stewart's 1965 Italian GP win came in only his eighth F1 race, and he finished third overall in his debut season. He went on to win three World Championships (1969, 1971, and 1973), and it could have been more, had it not been for the stomach ulcers that curtailed his 1972 season and his retirement at the end of the following year after the death of his teammate and friend, François Cevert. Stewart became a passionate and outspoken campaigner for driver safety after a crash at Spa in 1966 that left him trapped in his car for 25 minutes. His record tally of 27 wins in only 99 Grand Prix was outstanding and was only overtaken by Alain Prost in 1987. Stewart has since carved out a highly successful career as a commentator in the United States, and in 1997, he returned to F1 in partnership with his son, Paul. Stewart was awarded a knighthood by the Queen of England for his achievements in 2001.

▲ *Jackie Stewart gives a thumbs-up from the cockpit of his Tyrrell during the 1973 Italian GP at Monza, a race in which he finished fourth.*

◄ *In 1964, A. J. Foyt won ten out of 13 races, including the Indy 500, on his way to winning the USAC Championship.*

A. J. FOYT
U.S., BORN 1935

Anthony Joseph Foyt raced all types of four-wheeled vehicles, from midget, dirt-track, and sports cars to NASCARs and IndyCars. He was one of the most mentally and physically tough racers ever on the U.S. scene and made a number of astonishing comebacks after horrific accidents. He became the first four-time winner of the Indy 500 in 1977, having last won it in 1967. He rarely raced outside of North America, but won the Le Mans 24 Hours in 1967. Foyt remains the only driver to have won that race and the Daytona and Indy 500s. He also holds the record of most IndyCar victories (67) and most starts at the Indy 500 (35). Since retiring in 1993, he has made his name as an IndyCar team owner.

MICHELLE MOUTON
FRANCE, BORN 1951

Michelle Mouton was the first woman to make a major impact in the world of top-class rallying. After winning French rally championships in the 1970s, she burst onto the world scene when she became the first woman to claim a WRC victory at the 1981 San Remo Rally. The following year, she drove for the Audi works team and swept aside the opposition, winning the Acropolis, Portugal, and Brazil rallies, scoring 97 points, and only narrowly losing the WRC title to the German driver Walter Röhrl. Mouton's reputation was further enhanced when she finished second in the 1983 Pikes Peak Hill Climb and then won the event in 1985, setting a new record of 11 minutes, 25.39 seconds. After retiring from rally driving in 1986, she became a coorganizer of the Race of Champions (see p. 48).

▼ Michelle Mouton won four rallies during the eight years that she contested the World Rally Championship, from 1979 to 1986.

◄ Emerson Fittipaldi celebrates after winning the 1993 Indianapolis 500.

EMERSON FITTIPALDI
BRAZIL, BORN 1946

Fittipaldi moved to Europe in 1969, where he rapidly rose up through the ranks, driving Lotus cars in Formula Three, Formula Two, and, finally, Formula One. In 1972, he became F1's youngest World Championship winner and was the runner-up the following year. A move to McLaren in 1974 saw him win another world title, delighting fans with his fast, smooth driving style and gracious manner. After an unsuccessful stint with his brother's Copersucar F1 team, he left racing in 1980. However, his 1984 return in the U.S. saw him win the CART Championship in 1989 and two Indy 500s, in 1989 and 1993.

ALAIN PROST
FRANCE, BORN 1955

Often the quickest and frequently the smartest driver on the F1 circuit, Prost was signed by McLaren on the strength of a handful of test laps and successes in junior competitions, including the 1973 world karting title. After a difficult 1980 season, Prost joined Renault, with whom he finished fifth, fourth, and second in the championship, falling an agonizing two points behind Nelson Piquet in 1983. Prost rejoined McLaren and won three World Championships (1985, 1986, and 1989), earning the nickname "the Professor" for his precise, calculating driving style. The contrast between Prost and the aggressive, emotional, and sometimes reckless Ayrton Senna enthralled Formula One fans right up until Prost's retirement in 1993 after winning, in a Williams car, his fourth world title. With 51 F1 wins and 106 top-three finishes in 199 starts, Prost's record is extraordinary. He was also the World Championship runner-up four times, each time by the small margin of seven points or less.

▼ Alain Prost sits in his Williams car at the 1993 South African GP. Despite falling behind Ayrton Senna and Michael Schumacher in a bad start, the patient Frenchman reeled them both in to win the race.

JEFF GORDON

U.S., BORN 1971

Gordon was a motor-racing prodigy. Driving quarter midget cars in the U.S., he won 35 races and the Western States Championship at the age of six. Moving into karting and midget cars, he became the youngest U.S. National Midget champion at the age of 19 and moved full-time into NASCAR's Busch Series in 1991. Rookie of the Year in 1993, Gordon recorded his first top-class win at the 1994 Coca-Cola 600 and became the youngest-ever Winston Cup Series champion in 1995, aged 24. Three further championships and an average of almost six race wins per season make him one of the very best NASCAR drivers.

GIUSEPPE FARINA

ITALY, 1906–1966

The first-ever Formula One world champion in 1950, Farina had reached his driving peak in the late 1930s, when he won three Italian Drivers' Championships in a row (1937–1939). Farina's six-year F1 record (1950–1955) saw him take an exceptional 20 podium finishes in 33 races. After a series of bad accidents, he retired in 1955. Tragically, considering how dangerous motor racing was in his era, he was killed in a road accident on his way to watch the 1966 French GP.

BARRY SHEENE

U.K., 1950–2003

A popular celebrity who was an inspiration to many people involved in motorsports, Sheene was famous for his playboy lifestyle off the track and his fearless riding on it. Sheene won his first major honor, the British 750cc title, in 1970. A spectacular 167mph (270km/h) crash at Daytona in 1975 saw him break his left thigh, right arm, two ribs, and his collarbone. Yet he was back racing again only five weeks later. Riding for Suzuki, he won back-to-back GP500 World Championships in 1976 and 1977. Losing the title the following year to Kenny Roberts, Sheene battled against the American until 1982, when a crash during a practice for the British GP effectively ended his chances as a contender. He retired two years later.

▲ *Jeff Gordon's pit crew springs into action during the Brickyard 400 at Indianapolis, Indiana, in 2004. He went on to win the race for a record fourth time.*

▼ *British motorcycle legend Barry Sheene leans into a bend on his Suzuki in 1979. At one stage in his career, Sheene had 28 metal pins in his legs.*

►► *Parnelli Jones, in car number 115, takes a bend during the 1968 Riverside Motor Trend 500 at the Riverside Raceway.*

▲ *In his final race before his retirement, Tommi Makinen gets airborne during the 2003 Wales Rally GB.*

▼ *Michael Schumacher speeds to victory at the 2004 European GP. After winning the F1 drivers' title in 2000, Schumacher spent a remarkable 1,813 days as the world number one.*

TOMMI MAKINEN
FINLAND, BORN 1964

Makinen began his racing career competing in farm tractor events in Finland and became the national champion in 1982 and 1985. He entered his first rally in 1985 in a Ford Escort RS2000, and two years later, he made his debut in a WRC event, driving a Lancia. Moving to Ford in 1994, he won his first WRC event that year (the Rally of Finland) and was signed by Mitsubishi's Ralliart team. In seven years with Mitsubishi, Makinen won an unparalleled four WRC titles in a row (1996–1999) and finished third and fifth twice in the other three seasons. In 2002, he switched to Subaru for two seasons, notched up his 24th WRC win, and then announced his retirement.

PARNELLI JONES
U.S., BORN 1933

Rufus Parnell Jones was a hot rod racer who was offered a drive in major racing by millionaire J. C. Agajanian in 1960. Debuting at the Indy 500 the following year, Jones finished 12th and was named Rookie of the Year. In 1962, he became the first driver to break the 150mph (240km/h) barrier during qualifying, finishing fifth in the race. The 1963 Indy 500 was controversial for Jones. Leading by more than 20 seconds and with less than 100 miles (160km) to go, his car started spraying oil onto the track. The marshals allowed him to continue, and he won the race. After retiring, he enjoyed some success as a team boss, seeing Al Unser, Sr. win the Indy 500 for his team in 1970 and 1971.

MIKE HAWTHORN
U.K., 1929–1959

Hawthorn proved to be competitive in his early F1 career as a Ferrari driver. He also won the 1955 Le Mans, and, in 1958—despite only winning one race and enduring the death of his teammate, Peter Collins, at the German GP—a series of consistent drives saw him beat Stirling Moss to the F1 world title. Tragically, he was killed in a road accident shortly after retiring.

MICHAEL SCHUMACHER
GERMANY, BORN 1969

Few drivers get to start in 84 Grand Prix, but Michael Schumacher has won that many (by the end of 2005) in a glorious F1 career that has brought him an unprecedented seven World Championships. He was the German national adult kart champion at 17 and followed that with a short stint in Formula Three and sports cars. Schumacher made his Formula One debut in 1991 for Jordan, qualifying as an impressive seventh. Weeks later, he was hired by Benetton, for whom he finished third in his first full season and fourth in 1993, before becoming the world champion in both 1994 and 1995. Moving to Ferrari, he endured several less successful years and missed six races in 1999 with a broken leg. But in 2000, he gave Ferrari their first World Drivers' Championship since 1979. With the exception of 2003, which went to the last race, the next four years saw Schumacher and Ferrari utterly dominant. He won nine races in 2001, 11 races in 2002, and 13 out of 18 in 2004, winning an incredible five titles in a row. An absolute perfectionist, the German legend's extraordinary attention to technical details, extreme mental toughness, and physical fitness have set him apart from other drivers as he has broken almost every major F1 record.

DON "BIG DADDY" GARLITS
U.S., BORN 1932

Drag racing's leading pioneer, the Florida-born Garlits won the first drag race that he entered (the 1955 NHRA Safety Safari). Over forty years of racing, he built 34 dragsters (all named Swamp Rat) that powered him to an astonishing 144 major race victories and 17 national championships. He won the AHRA World Championship a record of ten times and was also IHRA World Champion five times. An excellent technical innovator, Garlits was the first to use air spoilers on a dragster. In 1971, he introduced the first successful rear-engine dragster, a design that has since become the standard. In 1975, he was the first drag racer to break the 250mph (400km/h) barrier, having broken the 200mph (320km/h) record 11 years earlier.

▲ At the 1986 Top Fuel world finals, Don Garlits performs a burnout to heat up his tires at the start line.

JOEY DUNLOP
U.K., 1952–2000

A true people's champion, modest and loved by his many fans, Dunlop first raced the Isle of Man Tourist Trophy (TT) in 1976. He went on to win a staggering 27 TT races in different classes. He won more than 160 events in British and Irish road racing, as well as an incredible five TT Formula One World Championships in a row (1982–1986). Away from the track, Dunlop did a lot deal of charity work, filling his race van with clothing and food and driving across Europe to help people in Romania and Bosnia. In 2000, Dunlop was leading a 125cc race in Estonia when he crashed his motorcycle and died instantly.

▲ Joey Dunlop rides to victory in the ultra-lightweight class of the Isle of Man TT in June 2000.

MIKA HAKKINEN
FINLAND, BORN 1968

After success in karting, Hakkinen entered and won the British Formula Three Championship in 1990. A drive in Formula One with Lotus followed, before he moved to McLaren as the third driver behind Ayrton Senna and Michael Andretti. When Andretti returned to the U.S. in 1993, the ice-cool Finn got his chance and out-qualified Senna in his first race. He showed great promise, collecting five third places and one second place in 1994, but an accident at the 1995 Australian GP almost cost him his life. By the late 1990s, Hakkinen appeared to be the only driver with the temperament and skills to counter the onslaught of Michael Schumacher. He won back-to-back World Championships in 1998 and 1999, but another accident in Australia, this time in 2001, saw him stay out for a year, which appeared to turn into full retirement. He sat out 2003 and 2004, but he returned to racing in 2005 and 2006, competing in German touring car events.

▼ Mika Hakkinen leads the field at the 1999 Spanish GP in Barcelona. Hakkinen won by 6.2 seconds over his McLaren teammate, David Coulthard.

JACK BRABHAM
AUSTRALIA, BORN 1926

Jack Brabham remains the only driver to have won an F1 World Championship in a car of his own design. Driving for Cooper, he won his first Grand Prix in 1959 at Monaco and followed that with the 1959 and 1960 Formula One World Championships. In 1962, he joined forces with Ron Tauranac to develop his own cars, and in 1966, he won four Grand Prix and his third world title, driving a self-designed Brabham-Repco BT19. In recognition of his services to motorsports, Brabham was knighted by the Queen of England in 1979.

▶ Australian Jack Brabham puts his self-designed Brabham BT3 Climax through its paces during the 1962 German GP at Nürburgring.

JOCHEN RINDT
AUSTRIA, 1941–1970

Throughout the 1960s, Rindt struggled to get a truly competitive drive in Formula One, although his daredevil racing style brought him a lot of success in Formula Two, winning both British

▲ Jochen Rindt focuses before the 1970 Dutch GP.

and French championships and 12 of the 19 European F2 races that he entered. He also caused a major surprise in 1965 when he won the Le Mans 24 Hours in a Ferrari 275LM with Pierre Masten. Rindt finally got a drive to match his talents in 1970, when he won five F1 races in a Lotus. Increasingly concerned about safety following the death of his friends Bruce McLaren and Piers Courage, Rindt was practicing for the Italian GP when he crashed and was killed close to the spot where his great hero, the German racer Count Wolfgang von Trips, died in 1961. No one beat his points total, and he became the only F1 world champion to be crowned after his death.

ANGEL NIETO
SPAIN, BORN 1947

At the age of 22, Angel Nieto became the first Spaniard to win a motorcycling world title when he became the 1969 50cc world champion. Throughout his long and incredibly successful career, he concentrated on riding smaller bikes— 50cc, 80cc, and 125cc—with great success. He won a total of six World Championships in the 50cc class and took seven world crowns in the 125cc class, including four in a row from 1981 to 1984. In total, Nieto won an astounding 90 Grand Prix races before retiring in 1986.

STIRLING MOSS
U.K., BORN 1929

The greatest driver never to win the Formula One World Championship, Stirling Crauford Moss was born into a motor racing family, and both his father Alfred and his mother Aileen were enthusiastic motorsports competitors. Moss made his name in Formula 500 (the forerunner of Formula Three) immediately after World War II and entered Grand Prix racing with the HWM team in 1951. He also entered the Monte Carlo Rally in 1952, coming in second. In 1955, Moss raced alongside the great Juan Manuel Fangio in the Mercedes works team. It was a glorious year, as he became the first British driver to win his home F1 Grand Prix and the first British winner of the Mille Miglia. He also won the Tourist Trophy, the Targa Florio, and finished second in the F1 World Championship. Frustratingly, he finished second in the next three championships and third in the two after that. He retired in 1962 after a serious crash at Goodwood, but his

outstanding sportsmanship, versatility, and racing prowess ensured that he has remained popular to this day. In a career in which he sat behind the wheel of more than 80 different vehicles, Moss won a truly incredible 194 of the 497 races that he entered between 1948 and 1962. In 2000, he was awarded a knighthood.

BOBBY ALLISON
U.S., BORN 1937

Part of the "Alabama Gang" that included his brother Donnie, Red Farmer, and Neil Bonnett, Allison had an aggressive driving style that saw him notch up a total of 84 NASCAR victories (putting him in third place beside Darryl Waltrip on the list of all-time wins). Finishing as the runner-up in five Winston Cup Series, he finally won the competition in 1983. In 1988, he won his third and last Daytona 500, just ahead of his son Davey, but a near-fatal crash at the Miller High Life 500 at Pocono later that year ended his racing career. Further tragedy struck the family when one son, Clifford, died during a practice for a NASCAR race in 1992 and the other son, Davey, died in a helicopter crash in 1993.

▲
Bobby Allison celebrates winning the 1988 Daytona 500 in his Buick.

▼ Racing a Maserati 250F, Stirling Moss defends his position from Alberto Ascari's Ferrari 625 during the Italian GP at Monza in 1954.

MARIO ANDRETTI
U.S., BORN 1940

A name that has been associated with motor racing on both sides of the Atlantic Ocean, Andretti and his twin brother Aldo were Italian immigrants who turned to sprint and midget car racing in the U.S. Aldo stopped racing after a severe accident, but Mario continued and prospered. He finished third in his first Indy 500 in 1965 (an event that he won four years later), won the Daytona 500 in 1967, and claimed three Champ Car National Championship trophies in the 1960s (his fourth came in 1984). Andretti spent a number of seasons in Formula One, regularly crossing the Atlantic to compete in U.S. competitions at the same time. In 1978, driving the Lotus 78 and 79 cars, he won six F1 Grand Prix and the World Title. To highlight his versatility, four years earlier, he had won the National Dirt Track title in the U.S. Andretti remained competitive right up to the end of his career, with his 52nd Champ Car victory coming at the 1993 Phoenix 200 at the age of 53 and a second-place finish in the 1995 Le Mans 24 Hours. In his sixties, Andretti could not resist trying out a car from his son's team during a practice for the 2003 Indy 500. The car flipped into the air, and Andretti was lucky to emerge relatively unharmed from the wreckage. That was it—the legend had finally finished with racing.

JOHN SURTEES
U.K., BORN 1934

John Surtees accomplished something that no other racer has done—win world championships on two wheels and on four. Riding MV Agusta bikes in the 1950s, he triumphed as the 500cc world champion four times and also took three 350cc crowns. He made his Formula One debut in a Lotus in 1960 and raced for Cooper and Lola before joining Ferrari in 1963. The following year, he beat Graham Hill by one point to win the World Drivers' Championship—an awesome achievement in motorsports history.

▲ In his last drive before his retirement, the 63-year-old veteran Mario Andretti tests the Andretti Racing Honda Dallara in preparation for the Indianapolis 500 in 2003.

◄ John Surtees practicing for the Italian GP on the famous Monza track near Milan in August 1957. Three years later, he was racing in Formula One cars.

► Carl "Foggy" Fogarty, on his Ducati 916SP, waves the British flag after winning a World Superbike race at Donington Park, U.K., in May 1995.

CARL FOGARTY
U.K., BORN 1965

The most successful World Superbike rider in history with 59 race wins, "Foggy" first raced in motocross when he was a boy. After winning the TT Formula One World Championship with Honda twice, he switched to Ducati in 1992 and recorded his first World Superbike win at the British GP, held at Donington Park. Between 1993 and 1999, he twice finished as the runner-up in World Superbikes but won the title four times (1994–1995 and 1998–1999). At Australia's Phillip Island Circuit in 2000 (the place where he won his first Superbike world title), Fogarty crashed, injured his shoulder and arm, and was forced to retire. He has stayed in Superbikes, managing a new team, Foggy Petronas Racing.

JIM CLARK
U.K., 1936–1968

While best known for his polished driving style and success in Formula One, Jim Clark proved to be a contender in almost every vehicle class that he entered. Having begun his racing career in local Scottish rallies, Clark joined the Lotus F1 team in 1960. Three years later, he won five nonChampionship races and a staggering seven Grand Prix to secure his first World Championship. His second came in 1965, and in 72 Grand Prix in total, Clark notched 25 wins and 33 pole positions. In 1963, he impressed everyone in his first attempt on the Indy 500 by finishing second, and two years later, he won the prestigious event. He died at the peak of his powers in a Formula Two race at Hockenheim in 1968.

ALAN JONES
AUSTRALIA, BORN 1946

Alan Jones was the no-nonsense driver who helped establish Williams as a force in Formula One. As a youngster, Jones worked in the car dealership of his father, Stan, who had himself been the winner of the 1959 Australian GP. He arrived in Great Britain in 1970 and struggled in the early part of the decade, but wins in Formula Three and Formula Atlantic led to F1 drives with Hesketh, Embassy Hill, Surtees, and Shadow before a move to Williams. Four Grand Prix wins in 1979 were followed by five wins and the World Title in 1980. Retiring after a mechanically-bad 1981 season, Jones made two brief comebacks (with Arrows in 1983 and Haas-Lola in 1985–1986) before returning to his home country.

JACKY ICKX
BELGIUM, BORN 1945

Ickx raced saloon cars before rapidly rising through Formula Three and Formula Two. In 1969 for Brabham and in 1970 for Ferrari, the popular Belgian finished second in the F1 World Championship. Battling with less and less effective Ferrari vehicles, he switched to Lotus in 1974 and then raced the remainder of the 1970s for a range of teams, completing his 116th and last Grand Prix in a Ligier. Ickx's racing career was incredibly varied. He won the Bathurst 1,000 in 1977, the Spa 24 Hours in 1966, Le Mans an outstanding six times (1969, 1975–1977, 1981–1982), the World Sports Car Championship (1982–1983), and the Dakar Rally in 1983. Today, Ickx often appears as a driver at historic events and has even raced against his daughter, Vanina.

▼ The legendary Scottish racing driver Jim Clark, pictured at Crystal Palace, England, in June 1965.

►► Belgian driver Jacky Ickx competing in his Tyrrell-Matra MS7 Ford in the 1967 German Formula Two GP at Nürburgring.

◀ Stéphane Peterhansel plunges his Mitsubishi down a sand dune during the eighth stage of the 2004 Dakar Rally, between Atar and Tidjika in Mauritania.

STÉPHANE PETERHANSEL

FRANCE, BORN 1965

A true phenomenon in the world of off-road racing, Peterhansel first rode a motorcycle at the age of eight and entered his debut motocross race at 16. Riding Yamaha motorcycles, he triumphed in the 1991 Dakar Rally and then dominated the 1990s, winning a further five times (1992–1993, 1995, and 1997–1998), while also adding the 1997 World Enduro Championship. In 1999, he made a surprise switch to cars and came in seventh in that year's Dakar race. He had an excellent season in 2004, winning the rallies of Morocco and Tunisia, and becoming only the second person after Hubert Auriol to have won the Dakar on both two wheels and four. He finished first again in 2005 with his codriver, Jean-Paul Cottet.

KENNY ROBERTS

U.S., BORN 1951

Roberts entered the U.S. National Motorcycling Championships at the age of 21 and went on to win 47 American Motorcyclist Association (AMA) National races in a wide range of classes. He won the AMA Grand National Championship in 1973 and 1974 and the prestigious Daytona 200 three times. In 1977, he dominated the AMA Formula One season, winning six out of seven races. He carried this into the GP500 World Championship where, in 1978, he became the first American 500cc champion. Roberts won the title in the following two seasons and retired in 1983. The oldest of his two sons, Kenny, Jr., won the GP500 world title in 2000—making them the first-ever father and son champions.

▲ Kenny Roberts of the U.S. holds the winner's trophy at the 1978 British GP, held at Silverstone.

BERND ROSEMEYER
GERMANY, 1909–1938

Bernd Rosemeyer's top-class racing career only lasted two and a half seasons. Yet the charismatic and extremely fast German made a great impact on the public, helped by his marriage to the famous aviator Elly Beinhorn. He came into four-wheeled racing on the back of hill-climb and grass-track success riding BMW and NSU motorbikes and gained a contract with the Auto Union team. He drove the tricky Auto Union cars like no one else could, fearlessly sliding them through corners like a motorcycle. Rosemeyer's record in Grand Prix races is astonishing, with ten victories in just 31 races.

At the age of 28, he was tragically killed while attempting a speed record on a stretch of highway between Frankfurt and Darmstadt.

GILLES VILLENEUVE
CANADA, 1950–1982

Villeneuve was the Canadian snowmobile racing champion before coming into prominence in Formula Atlantic racing. Obtaining his first Formula One drive with McLaren in 1977, he became a full-time F1 driver the following year, replacing Niki Lauda at Ferrari, where he spent the rest of his career. Although he only recorded six wins out of 67 Grand Prix starts, Villeneuve's impact went beyond his victories and his 1979 World Championship runner-up place. His dashing, flamboyant style was very popular with fans, who were shocked by his death during qualifying for the 1982 Belgian GP. His son Jacques became F1 world champion in 1997.

▲ *Gilles Villeneuve drives his Ferrari 312 T2 in 1978, the year in which he won his first Grand Prix, at his home track in Canada.*

◀◀ *The most successful member of IndyCars' greatest racing dynasty, Al Unser, Sr. drives his Parnelli car at Canada's Mosport Park in 1977.*

AL UNSER, SR.
U.S., BORN 1939

No less than six members of the Unser family have raced in the Indy 500, recording nine victories between them. Al Unser, Sr., the younger brother of Bobby and father of Al Unser, Jr., is the most successful, with four Indy 500 crowns, three championships (1970, 1983, 1985), and 39 wins. Starting in modified roadsters and sprint cars, Unser first raced the Pikes Peak Hill Climb in 1960, finishing second to his brother Bobby. In 1964, he made his IndyCar debut, and the following year, he debuted at the Indy 500, finishing ninth despite starting on the back row. Unser went on to lead 644 laps at the Indy 500—more than any other driver. In 1970, he won the USAC National Championship, winning ten races on oval, road, and dirt tracks, but his 1972 bid to become the first winner of three Indy 500s in a row failed narrowly. He retired in 1994, after struggling to qualify for his 28th Indy 500.

NIGEL MANSELL
U.K., BORN 1953

Nothing came easy to Nigel Mansell. It took more than 70 Grand Prix with Lotus and Williams before he recorded his first F1 race win, and in 1986, he seemed on the verge of the world title when he suffered a spectacular puncture in the last race of the season and finished second. He was the runner-up again in 1987 and 1991. A prickly character, Mansell was an out-and-out racer with a reputation for daring overtaking moves that endeared him to fans. The F1 Championship was finally his in 1992, when he scored almost double the amount of points of second-placed Ricardo Patrese. Yet, Williams did not renew his contract, and he moved to IndyCar racing, winning the CART Championship at his first attempt. A brief return to Formula One saw his 31st and last win come with a stunning drive at the 1994 Australian GP.

▲ *Nigel Mansell prepares to start the 1990 Italian GP for Ferrari. Mansell endured many crashes and injuries during his career, including a broken neck and second-degree burns to his bottom from a fuel leak.*

DANICA SUE PATRICK LEADS THE INDY 500

At the 2005 Indianapolis 500, Danica Sue Patrick became only the fourth woman (after Janet Guthrie, Lyn St. James, and Sarah Fisher) to take part in the famous race. She then became the first female driver to lead the race, which she did for a total of 19 laps before being overtaken six laps from the finish line, when she had to slow down to conserve fuel. Patrick's fourth-place finish was the highest by a woman at the Indy 500, and she followed that result with two pole positions later in the season, at Kansas and Kentucky. Only a few women have achieved success at the highest levels of motorsports. These include Michelle Mouton in rallying, drag racing's Shirley Muldowney, 2001 Dakar Rally winner Jutta Kleinschmidt, and Lella Lombardi—the only woman to secure a top-six finish in a Formula One race. Patrick is part of a new generation of female racers that includes Sarah Fisher and Katherine Legge, who, in 2005, became the first woman to win an open-wheel race in North America, in the Toyota Atlantic Championship.

► *Danica Sue Patrick, driving for Team Rahal, makes history as the first woman to lead the Indy 500 in May 2005.*

◄ Before moving to the Indy Racing League, Danica Sue Patrick became the first woman to achieve a podium finish in the 30-year history of the Toyota Atlantic Championship, when she finished third at Monterrey, Mexico, in 2003.

GREAT TEAMS

Over the years, some extraordinary vehicles have been produced by the leading motor-racing teams. Some have been highly innovative, breathtakingly beautiful, or astonishingly successful. Here, we look at several of the major teams, the success that they have enjoyed, and the machines that they have produced.

JAGUAR

Founded as the Swallow Sidecar Company in 1922, Jaguar (renamed in 1935) emerged as a major manufacturer of luxury sports vehicles shortly before World War II, with its SS100 enjoying wins in the Alpine and RAC rallies. The XK120, with a top speed in excess of 117mph (190km/h), was the fastest production car in the world when it was unveiled in 1949. It won a number of races and rallies and took the top four places in the 1951 Rallye du Soleil. The famous Jaguar C-Type, which was just designed for racing, shared many similarities with the XK120, but was lighter and much more

▼ *Having won in 1988, a Jaguar XJR-9LM races at the 1989 Le Mans 24 Hours. The car weighed 1,950 lbs. (881kg) and had a powerful 6.995-liter engine that generated 750 horsepower.*

powerful. It scored Le Mans 24 Hours victories in 1951 and 1953. Its successor, the D-Type, had a top speed of more than 167mph (270km/h) and won the 12 Hours of Sebring in 1955. Le Mans 24 Hours wins in 1955 and 1956 were followed by a sweep of the top four places by D-Types at the 1957 event. After an official break of almost 30 years, Jaguar returned to racing in 1982 and won the European Touring Car Championship in 1984. Its sixth Le Mans 24 Hours win came in 1988 with an XJR-9LM that was capable of more than 241mph (390km/h). That year also saw Jaguar win the Daytona 24 Hours and the World Sports Car Championship. At the start of this century, Jaguar dominated the Trans-Am Series, with championship wins in 2001, 2003, 2004, and 2005.

▼ *An elegant Jaguar C-Type is raced at a meeting in 2002. Just 54 C-Types and 53 D-Types were manufactured by Jaguar.*

PRODRIVE

Prodrive was founded in 1984 by Ian Parry and rally codriver David Richards. The company began in rallying and has grown into one of the biggest businesses in motorsports. In its first year, Prodrive formed the Rothmans Porsche team, winning seven different rallies and coming second in the European Rally Championship. Forming a powerful partnership with Subaru in 1990, Prodrive won three WRC manufacturers' titles in a row (1995–1997) and gave Colin McRae a memorable drivers' title in 1995. By the end of 2005, the team had won more than 130 international rallies, as well as six WRC

manufacturers' or drivers' titles. In 2003, a Prodrive team entered the Australian V8 Supercar Championship for the first time, and another won the GTS class at the Le Mans 24 Hours. Having run the BAR Formula One team between 2002 and 2004, Prodrive is planning to enter its own F1 team in 2008.

WILLIAMS

Frank Williams founded Williams Grand Prix Engineering in 1977 with Patrick Head, a talented engineer. Three years later, they celebrated a double win, taking the constructors' title and seeing Alan Jones win the World Drivers' Championship. Williams won another drivers' crown in 1982 with Keke Rosberg and three more constructors' titles in 1981, 1986, and 1987. A car accident in 1986 left Frank Williams paralyzed, but his appetite for racing remained undiminished, and the 1990s was Williams' finest decade. It began with the

In 1992, Nigel Mansell claimed nine victories and the Formula One drivers' title in the Williams FW14B.

FW14B car that took Nigel Mansell to the title in 1992. This was the first of four drivers' championships and five constructors' titles won by Williams in the 1990s. Frank Williams has never been afraid to put team demands ahead of his drivers and famously fired Nigel Mansell, Alain Prost, and Damon Hill after they had won titles. One of F1's biggest players, the team had a total of 113 Grand Prix wins by the end of 2005.

HENDRICK MOTORSPORTS

Formed as All Star Racing by Rick Hendrick, the team entered NASCAR in 1984 and won almost immediately, with Geoff Bodine claiming the Sovran Bank 500. The mid 1990s was a golden period, as Hendrick became the only team to have won four Winston Cups in a row (1995–1998). Another championship win came in 2001. Of the five cars raced by the team, Jeff Gordon's number 24 has been by far the most successful, with 73 Winston/Nextel Cup victories by the end of 2005. The team suffered a terrible tragedy in October 2004, however, when a plane carrying family and senior members of the team crashed, killing all ten people on board. Later that day, Jimmie Johnson won the Subway 500 race for Hendrick. The team put the tragedy behind it in 2005, winning ten Nextel Cup races, including the Daytona 500.

Subaru's Petter Solberg (left) celebrates with Prodrive's technical director, David Lapworth, after winning a stage of the 2004 Rally of Italy.

Hendrick Motorsports' Jeff Gordon is pushed into the pit by his team. Gordon had run out of fuel after winning the Auto Club 500 race at the California Speedway in May 2004.

▲ Enzo Ferrari, pictured here in 1953, had been a driver for Alfa Romeo before founding his own race team. He died in 1988 at the age of 90.

FERRARI

Ferrari is known throughout the world for its excellent, high-performance cars, passionate fans, and red "Rosso Corsa" racing colors. Its founder, Enzo Ferrari, formed the Scuderia Ferrari team that handled Alfa Romeo's racing entries from 1929. In the late 1930s, Ferrari split from Alfa and began building its own cars. The first successful model was the Tipo 125, which first raced in 1947 and took part in the inaugural Formula One season in 1950. Ferrari quickly became a force in F1 racing, with World Drivers' Championship titles in 1952, 1953, 1956, and 1958. Over the next 20 years, the company reinforced its reputation, producing a succession of outstanding vehicles that competed in GT, sports, and endurance racing. Ferrari cars and drivers have won the Targa Florio seven times, the Mille Miglia eight times, and the Le Mans 24 Hours nine times. A relatively unsuccessful 15 years in Formula One ended with the arrival of Jean Todt as the team boss in 1993 and driver Michael Schumacher in 1996. Schumacher transformed the team, with a staggering five world drivers' titles (2000–2004) and six constructors' titles (1999–2004) in a row. Ferrari now leads the sport, with the most F1 race wins (184 by the end of 2005) and most constructors' championships (14).

▼ The sleek Ferrari 330 P3/4 stunned race fans by taking the top three places at the Daytona 24 Hours in 1967.

▲ Team Penske driver Sam Hornish, Jr. exits from the pit during the Miami Indy 300, round one of the 2005 Indy season.

PENSKE

Roger Penske retired from race driving in 1965 to form Penske Racing and Team Penske. Success came almost immediately, with wins in the Trans-Am Series Championship in 1968 and 1969 and victory at the 1969 Daytona 24 Hours. In the 1970s, Penske entered NASCAR and F1 racing, but tragedy struck when Mark Donohue, the team's engineer and driver, died during a practice for the 1975 Austrian F1 GP. The team's greatest success has come in Indy racing, with an extraordinary 13 Indy 500 victories. With more than 120 race wins and 11 national championships by the end of 2005, Penske is the most successful team in IndyCar history. After leaving NASCAR in 1980, Penske returned full-time in 1991. Driving the famous number 2 car, Rusty Wallace became a clear favorite with fans, recording 37 Nextel Cup wins for the team by the end of his "Last Call" season in 2005.

APRILIA

Aprilia began making mopeds and motorcycles in the 1960s and produced its first motocross bike, the Scarabeo, in 1970. After winning its first Italian Motocross Championship in 1977, Aprilia emerged internationally in the 1980s to enjoy road-racing success against the giants, Yamaha and Honda. From 1985 to 2004, Aprilia's success in smaller-engine championships was impressive, with 163 race victories, 472 podium finishes, and a total of 22 world titles. Since 1992, Aprilia bikes have won six 125cc World Championships and seven 250cc world titles, including a three-in-a-row triumph for Max Biaggi (1994–1996). The team has not matched this success at Superbike or MotoGP level, although parts of its innovative RS3 bike, such as throttle by wire, have been copied by other teams.

LOLA

Lola was formed by Eric Broadley, a quantity surveyor with a passion for building cars. The team debuted its first vehicle, the beautiful Mark I, in 1958. It became the first car to lap Brands Hatch in less than one minute. In the mid 1960s, Lola developed its legendary series of muscular T70 endurance cars, which won the Daytona 24 Hours as well as Can-Am and TT competitions. Lola cars enjoyed success in Indy racing too, with the first of three Indy 500 victories coming in 1966. The team sporadically entered Formula One, with little success, which is in contrast to its fortunes in CART (now Champ Car) racing. There, legends such as Mario Andretti, Bobby Rahal, Nigel Mansell, and Paul Tracy clocked up ten championship titles. In the 1990s, Lola provided the chassis for all of the cars entering the Formula 3,000 Championship and the CART Indy Lights Championship. The company was also chosen to supply the chassis for every car competing in the first A1 Grand Prix season, in 2005–2006.

◀◀ *Max Biaggi of Italy speeds to victory on his Aprilia in the 250cc race of the 1995 German GP at Nürburgring.*

▼ *The legendary Stirling Moss drives a Lola Mark I in a historic car race at Silverstone, U.K., in 2002.*

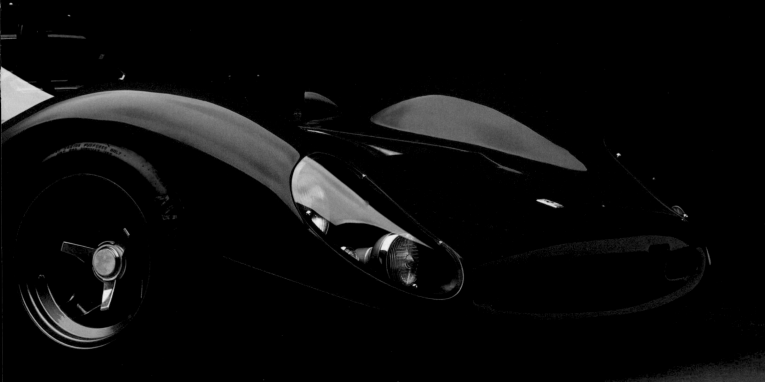

ROUSH RACING

Roush Racing was formed by Jack Roush in 1988. Roush had previously driven dragsters and worked for Ford, developing road-racing vehicles that enjoyed success in the Trans-Am Series. His team debuted in NASCAR's Winston Cup with car number 6, driven by a little-known short-track driver named Mark Martin. Since the early 1990s, Martin has almost always been at the top of the sport. He had scored 35 wins by the end of 2005 (out of Roush's total of 74), 359 top-ten finishes, and four runner-up positions in

▲ A delighted Jack Roush watches his drivers qualify for a 2005 Nextel Cup race.

▲ Matt Kenseth, in Roush Racing's number 17 car, races with teammate Greg Biffle during the 2005 Nextel Cup Series Banquet 400.

▼ Mick Doohan takes to the track on his 500cc Honda motorcycle for an exhibition ride in 1999.

▶▶ In October 2005, reigning 250cc world champion Daniel Pedrosa claimed Honda's 600th Grand Prix win, at Australia's Phillip Island Circuit.

the championship—but the title always eluded him. Roush finally got its first Nextel Cup crown in 2003, with Matt Kenseth, and won again in 2004, this time with Kurt Busch. The team also won the 2002 Busch Series and the 2000 Craftsman Truck Series. The team is well-known in the U.S. for its elimination competition, now televised as *Driver X*, where aspiring young NASCAR drivers compete on a series of tests and races for a place in the Roush team. Former winners include Robby Gordon, Kurt Busch, and, in 2004, Todd Kluever, who is scheduled to drive for Roush in the 2007 Nextel Cup.

HONDA

Honda's major racing debut was in 1959 at the Isle of Man TT. At the same location two years later, Mike Hailwood gave the team its first major victories, in the 125cc and 250cc classes. With the exception of withdrawing from racing for most of 1968 following the death of Jo Schlesser, Honda has always been present on the motorcycle-racing scene. It has had huge success in road

racing and off-road competitions, including a record 16 Baja 1,000 victories by the end of 2005. Honda has won eight AMA Superbike and five World Superbike riders' titles, yet had to wait until 1983 before securing the ultimate prize in motorcycle racing, when Freddie Spencer became the GP500 world champion. The team won three of the next ten competitions before embarking on an overpowering display of dominance as Mick Doohan and Valentino Rossi won nine out of ten titles for Honda from 1994 to 2003. In 2001, Rossi's win at Suzuka, Japan, gave the company its 500th Grand Prix win. Honda also has an important history in four-wheel racing, particularly in supplying engines. Honda-powered cars won 71 F1 Grand Prix by the end of 2005 and also won 14 out of 16 races in the 2004 IRL season. After taking control of the BAR F1 team, Honda Racing F1 raced the 2006 season with Jenson Button and Rubens Barrichello as its drivers.

PORSCHE

Dr. Ferdinand Porsche was famous as the engineer who designed Auto Union's Grand Prix cars, as well as the first Volkswagen car.

He set up his own company in 1931, and it began making its own racing cars in the late 1940s. Since then, Porsche cars have been extraordinarily successful, clocking up thousands of victories in a vast array of competitions, including the Le Mans 24 Hours (16 wins), the Daytona 24 Hours (20 wins), and the 12 Hours of Sebring (17 wins). In addition, Porsche cars have triumphed 11 times in the Targa Florio, won 20 European Hill Climbing Championships, and won the Dakar Rally in 1984 and 1986. A number of its cars, including the incredibly popular 911 and the powerful 917, have attained iconic status. In Formula One, the team is best known for providing engines to the McLaren team in the 1980s. These propelled both Niki Lauda and Alain Prost (twice) to the World Drivers' Championship.

McLaren

New Zealand driver Bruce McLaren founded his race team in 1963. McLaren died during testing for the Can-Am in 1970, but the team continued. A landmark year came in 1974, as the team won both the F1 World Drivers' Championship (with Emerson Fittipaldi) and the constructors' title. The second of a current total of 11 F1 drivers' titles followed in 1976. Ron Dennis took control of McLaren in 1981 and presided over a staggering period of achievement. Its MP4-2 is arguably the most successful F1 car ever, scoring 22 wins from 48 races and 329.5 championship points. In eight seasons between 1984 and 1991, McLaren won the World Drivers' Championship seven times—Niki Lauda was the champion in 1984, while Alain Prost and his rival Ayrton Senna each won several titles. During a period of F1 dominance by Williams and Ferrari, Mika Hakkinen won the world title in 1998 and 1999. Hakkinen's successor, Kimi Räikkönen, was narrowly beaten in 2005 by Renault's Fernando Alonso. Controversially, McLaren announced in late 2005 that they had hired Alonso for the 2007 season.

▲ McLaren mechanics inspect the Honda engine of Gerhard Berger's Formula One car at the 1990 Hungarian GP.

▲▲ Jo Siffert races a Porsche 917 at the 1971 Spa-Francorchamps 620-mile (1,000km) race. The 917/30 could reach 60mph (100km/h) in less than 2.3 seconds and had a top speed of more than 232mph (375km/h).

DOMINANCE

In many different classes of motorsports, there have been periods when one team or manufacturer has stood out—when a team and its combination of driver and machine has simply been better than the rest. Here are some examples of dominant teams and vehicles from a variety of different classes and eras.

▲ *A Bugatti Brescia, a forerunner of the mighty Type 35, rounds a corner on two wheels in the early 1920s.*

LONG REIGNS

Some vehicles are dominant for only one season. The Ferrari F2004, for example, won 15 out of 18 Formula One races in 2004, yet it struggled when a modified version was run at the start of 2005. Other cars, such as the Porsche 935, have longer careers. The 935 dominated sports and endurance racing, winning more than 150 races between 1976 and 1984, including six Daytona 24 Hours and six 12 Hours of Sebring. Some vehicles have achieved greatness in a range of racing classes. The Bugatti Type 35, for example, was considered to be one of the most exceptional racing cars. It competed in sprints, Grand Prix, long road races, and hill climbs from 1924 and won in all of those categories. Despite costing around $2,500 (the price of a house in London, England, at the time), the Type 35 was popular with wealthy amateur racers who clocked up more than 1,000 minor race victories in the machine. Type 35Bs and Cs had outstanding success in 1928 and 1929, when the cars won eight of the then Grand Prix, including the first Monaco GP in 1929. The car also won the exceptionally demanding Targa Florio five years in a row.

▼ *Swedish rally driver Bjorn Waldegaard takes his Lancia Stratos around a bend during the RAC Rally of Great Britain in November 1975.*

STAYING ON TOP

A stint at the top of racing can spur a team or manufacturer on to try to maintain their dominance. Italian manufacturer Lancia, for example, had a proud record in rallying, winning four World Rally Championship (WRC) constructors' titles in the 1970s, three of them with the team's Stratos car (of which less than 500 were built). The distinctive, sharp-edged Lancia Delta was first introduced in 1979 and was developed through the 1980s into the more powerful four-wheel-drive HF and Integrale versions. After winning their debut WRC race in 1987, Lancia Deltas completely overshadowed the opposition in not only that year, but for six seasons in a row, winning six consecutive World Constructors' Championships, plus an astonishing 46 victories from 66 rallies.

In the U.S., Chevrolet won its first NASCAR Grand National (the forerunner of the Winston and Nextel cups) with driver Buck Baker in 1957. The company went on to produce race cars for a number of teams, which, between them, won a further 28 NASCAR titles, including eight out of ten Winston Cups in the 1990s. The American automobile giant also provided the Chevrolet Monte Carlo in which Tony Stewart won the 2005 Nextel Cup crown.

◄ *Australia's Troy Bayliss wheelies his Ducati during a World Superbike race at Brands Hatch, U.K., in August 2000. Bayliss overtook Great Britain's Neil Hodgson on the final lap to win.*

►► *British racing legend Mike Hailwood speeds around a bend on his MV Agusta motorcycle at Brands Hatch in January 1965.*

▼ *Tony Smith drives an Alfa Romeo Tipo B (P3) at the Maserati Ferrari Festival in August 2002.*

MASTERFUL MOTORCYCLES

Dominance in motorsports is not always long-lasting. A pioneering design can be quickly overtaken by its rivals' models. In this context, Meccanica Verghera (MV) Agusta's supremacy at the top levels of motorcycle racing was extraordinary. The company was an industrial and aeronautics business that branched into motorcycles after World War II. Its founder, Count Domenico Agusta, was a racing fanatic who insisted on the best for his racing bikes, employing some of the world's top riders. MV Agusta won six World Championships in 125cc, two in 250cc, and ten in 350cc, but its real mark was made in the top-level 500cc class. Between 1958 and 1974, its silver and red machines (ridden by the likes of Giacomo Agostini, Mike Hailwood, John Surtees, and Phil Read) won all 17 World GP Championships. More recently, Ducati had a similar level of ascendency in World Superbikes. Since the championship started in 1988, Ducati won 13 of the 18 manufacturers' crowns and 11 riders' titles by the end of 2005. In 2003, the team won all 24 races and filled the top nine positions in the riders' championship.

DESIGNED FOR DOMINANCE

Considered to be one of the greatest of all of the racing car designers, Vittorio Jano was hired from Fiat by Alfa Romeo in 1923. Jano produced one of the stand-out racing-car designs in the form of the P2 the following year. The P2 won its debut race at the French GP in 1924 and also won many of the major races that it entered over the next few years. Jano then designed an unusual eight-cylinder engine (made out of two four-cylinder engines put together) and attached it to his elegant yet powerful Alfa 8C 2300. This car trounced the opposition at Le Mans, winning the 24 Hours race four times in a row (1931–1934) with four different driver combinations. Jano's true successor to the P2 was the P3 Monoposto, also known as the Tipo B. One of the first genuine single-seat racing cars, the P3 won the first race that it entered, the 1932 Italian Grand Prix, and almost every other major race that it contested in 1932 and 1933. The P3 famously provided the legendary Tazio Nuvolari with his greatest win of all when, at the 1935 German GP, he beat the mighty Silver Arrows cars of Auto Union and Mercedes on their home ground.

INNOVATIONS

Pioneering new technology can be essential to success in motorsports. In drag racing, for example, Don Garlits' innovations brought him huge success, while John Force won ten NHRA Funny Car World Championships in a row (1993–2002), by virtue of his team always remaining one step ahead of the opposition. Here are some other great motor-racing pioneers and their innovations.

▲ *Norm Hall drives a car powered by an Offenhauser engine in the Indy 500 in Indianapolis, Indiana, in 1965.*

▶▶ *Stig Blomqvist and codriver Bjorn Cederberg race their four-wheel-drive Audi Quattro A2 in the 1984 Acropolis Rally in Greece.*

▲ *John Force accelerates during the National Hot Rod Association (NHRA) Nationals at the Motor Speedway in Las Vegas, Nevada, in April 2000.*

OVAL-TRACK TRIUMPHS

The cars and engines that were designed and built by Harry Miller and Fred Offenhauser dominated U.S. oval-track racing in the 1920s. Traditionally, regular production car parts were adapted for racing car use, but Miller had almost every part made from scratch at his factory. Such attention to detail brought victories, but the cost contributed to Miller's bankruptcy in 1933. However, Offenhauser's influence as an engine designer continued. Between 1947 and 1964, every car that won the Indy 500 was powered by an Offenhauser, "Offy," engine. Five of those wins were in vehicles with "offset" engines designed by Frank Kurtis. Kurtis realized that an engine placed toward the side of the car that is closest to the inside of the track improved balance and handling. It also allowed riders to sit lower in the car, allowing for better aerodynamics.

FOUR-WHEEL DRIVE

Harry Miller produced the first four-wheel-drive car to enter a Grand Prix, in 1934, but the first ever was Jacobus Spijker's car, the Spyker, which won the Birmingham Motor Hill Climb in 1906. Later, the 1935 Alfa Bimotore transmitted engine power to both rear and front wheels from two engines, one at the front and one at the back. Four-wheel

drive also attracted a flurry of interest in Indy racing in the mid-1960s and Formula One in 1969, but in F1, only the Matra MS84 scored a single championship point. Audi unveiled its Quattro in 1980. This powerful four-wheel-drive car offered outstanding grip and traction in difficult conditions, making it an obvious rally contender. Its first outing at the Algarve Rally was as a non-competition car driven by Hannu Mikkola. Onlookers were stunned as the car posted a time that was 30 minutes faster than the competitors. The Quattro won two WRC manufacturers' titles (1982 and 1984) and two drivers' titles (1983–1984), national titles in four countries, and three consecutive Pikes Peak International Hill Climbs (1985–1987) for Michelle Mouton, Bobby Unser, and Walter Röhrl.

LOTUS

Alongside Vittorio Jano, Colin Chapman is considered to be one of the foremost racing-car designers and, arguably, Formula One's greatest innovator. Chapman formed Lotus in 1952, and his 1958 Lotus Elite was one of the first sports cars to feature a body made out of fiberglass. He also pioneered the use of struts as a rear suspension device on the Lotus 12 racing car. Today, these are widely used and are known as Chapman struts. In 1962, he produced the Lotus 25, the first F1 car to feature a monocoque body with a reclined driving position that was molded precisely for each driver—all features that are used today. With its sleek looks and low profile, the Lotus 25 generated less drag than its rivals and won the Formula One constructors' and drivers' titles in 1963. Lotus was also one of the first teams to adopt wings and other aerodynamic innovations that were designed to create downforce to help

▶ Jim Clark races the groundbreaking Lotus 25 to victory at the 1962 British GP, held at Aintree.

cars grip the track. In the 1970s, Chapman was an innovator in ground effect, used to create even more downforce. His Lotus 78 and 79 cars featured side skirts and a shaped underbody, creating an area of very low air pressure underneath the car. Combined with higher air pressure above, this forced the car down, making it "stick" to the road. Mario Andretti drove a Lotus 79 to the World Drivers' Championship in 1978, with his teammate Ronnie Peterson coming in second.

FORMULA ONE INNOVATIONS

Formula One has been at the cutting edge for a long time, with many of its vehicle and technology innovations later adopted by standard road vehicles. Some of F1's innovations appear strange, such as the six-wheeled cars that first emerged with the Tyrrell P34 in 1976. Other technical refinements,

such as carbon-fiber bodies and antilock brakes, have proved to be more successful. Computer-aided driving systems emerged in the late 1980s, reaching a peak in cars such as the Williams FW14B. Its equipment included active suspension, a semiautomatic transmission, and traction control to improve grip, especially at starts. Active suspension automatically alters the riding height of the car as it corners, brakes, and accelerates, making the most of a car's aerodynamics and maximizing its downforce. The car brought Nigel Mansell the 1992 World Drivers' Championship and Williams the constructors' title. Its successor, the FW15, driven by Alain Prost, won the 1993 championship, but many systems were banned at the end of that season because the cars were believed to be going too fast for safety.

▲ Mario Andretti stormed to victory in the debut race of the innovative Lotus 79 at the 1978 Belgian GP.

▲ Patrick Depailler races a six-wheeled Tyrrell P34 in 1976. The car only won one race, the Swedish GP, driven by Jody Scheckter.

◀◀ Colin Chapman (right) inspects an engine in the late 1960s. In the center is Graham Hill, who won the 1968 F1 world title for Lotus.

RIVALRIES

From Miller versus Duesenberg and Petty against Pearson in U.S. racing to Moss versus Fangio and Senna against Prost in F1, motorsports have produced some fascinating rivalries. These have existed between drivers, riders, manufacturers, and race teams.

▲ *In 1938, Tazio Nuvolari drove this Auto Union Type D to a historic win in the Donington GP in the U.K.*

▼ *Jochen Mass drives the 1954 Mercedes W196, capable of a top speed of 174mph (280km/h), at a historic car race in 2004.*

THE SILVER ARROWS

In 1934, the new chancellor of Germany, Adolf Hitler, offered German carmakers 500,000 Reichmarks a year to produce successful racing cars as a source of national pride. Mercedes-Benz and Auto Union did not disappoint him, as their legendary *Die Silberpfeile*—the "Silver Arrows"—swept away all before them in the prewar period. The rivalry between the two teams was passionate. In the Auto Union camp was Dr. Ferdinand Porsche, a truly great car engineer, while Mercedes was led by legendary team boss Alfred Neubauer. Neubauer was a pioneer of racing strategy, insisting on precisely

rehearsed routines for both drivers and pit crews and the use of trackside flags to communicate instructions. Neubauer was involved in the decision to strip the white paint off the Mercedes W25 in 1934, leaving the bare silver metal exposed in order to dip under the 1,650 lbs. (750kg) maximum weight for racing. Both Auto Union's and Mercedes' cars were highly streamlined and immensely powerful machines. The Mercedes W125 generated in excess of 600 horsepower, a figure not matched in Can-Am races until the late 1960s and in F1 until the early 1980s. With top speeds of more than 186mph (300km/h), the various Silver Arrows models tore the opposition apart in Grand Prix, hill climbs, and prestigious events, including the Coppa Acerbo and the Vanderbilt Cup. Mercedes produced a new Silver Arrow in 1954, before pulling out of motorsports at the end of the following year. But in the short period of time that the magical Mercedes W196 raced, it won nine of the 12 F1 Grand Prix that it entered.

WHEN TWO MAKES COLLIDE

The Silver Arrows period was only one of many occasions when several rival manufacturers have emerged to lead the pack. In the 1950s, great teams such as Ferrari, Maserati, Alfa Romeo, and Mercedes battled for Formula One supremacy, while there were epic battles in the 1960s between Ford GT40s and Ferraris in endurance racing, especially at Le Mans. In Australian racing, Ford and Holden have carried their long and intense rivalry into V8 Supercars, where fans are passionately divided by their colors—blue for Ford and red for Holden. Honda and Yamaha have dominated motorcycling since 1978. In both the GP500 World Championship and its successor, MotoGP, Honda riders have won the title 13 times compared to Yamaha's 11 (to the end of 2005). The only other manufacturer to win during this period has been Suzuki, with four titles.

CLASH OF THE TITANS

Many rivalries between drivers have been friendly away from the track. Stirling Moss' epic battles with Juan Manuel Fangio, for example, saw both drivers form a deep respect and friendship for each other. But other rivalries are very intense. Michael Schumacher's collision with Damon Hill at the 1994 Australian GP saw the German win the world title, but his relationship with the British driver was badly affected. In motorcycling, the rivalry between Italy's Max Biaggi and Valentino Rossi was so strong that Rossi did not even acknowledge Biaggi on his Web site, simply putting crosses in place of his name.

In 1989, arguably the fiercest rivalry ever seen in Formula One reached boiling point. McLaren teammates Alain Prost and Ayrton Senna were battling in the Japanese GP at Suzuka. Prost led, but Senna was fighting for a way through. With only six laps to go, the pair collided and crashed out of the race, leaving Prost to win the world title. Prost left McLaren for Ferrari, but a similar showdown occurred at the same circuit the following year. With Prost leading Senna, the pair crashed again, but this time it was Senna's turn to become the world champion.

THE FOX VS. THE KING

In NASCAR, rivalries have traditionally been part of the sport's appeal, but the greatest and longest was that between Dave Pearson, nicknamed "The Silver Fox," and Richard "The King" Petty. From the 1960s, the battle lasted for more than 550 races. The pair led the NASCAR field, ranking first and second in the list of all-time career wins and pole positions. Between 1963 and 1977, they finished first and second in a race 63 times. The epic rivalry peaked with a momentous finish at the 1976 Daytona 500. After trading the lead several times, the pair raced side by side during the final lap. Making contact coming out of turn four, they spun and crashed. Petty's car ended up on the grass just in front of the finish line, but the engine was dead. Despite sustaining more damage, Pearson's engine was still running, and he limped across the line to claim one of the most exciting victories in motorsports. Pearson went on to win a nine more races that year, more than any other driver.

◄◄ Holden and Ford cars battle it out during the Chinese round of the 2005 V8 Supercar Championship held at the Shanghai International Circuit.

◄ The Ford GT40, one of the great endurance cars. In 1966, the car claimed victories at both the Le Mans and Daytona 24 Hour races.

▲ At the 1967 National 500, NASCAR's most successful driver, Richard Petty (43), speeds past his fierce rivals Dave Pearson (17) and Mario Andretti (11) as they fight to regain control of their cars.

MICHAEL SCHUMACHER'S SEVENTH HEAVEN

Michael Schumacher has had a long and fruitful association with Belgium's magnificent Spa-Francorchamps Circuit. In 1991, it was the location of his surprise Formula One debut, standing in for the Jordan team's Bertrand Gachot, who was in prison. The following year, it was the scene of his first F1 Grand Prix win, driving for Benetton, and in 1996, the circuit on which he claimed his second victory for Ferrari. Together, the legendary Italian team and the masterful German driver dominated F1 racing at the start of this century, claiming five consecutive drivers' titles. In 2004, Schumacher blew away the opposition, winning the first five races, retiring at Monaco, and then winning an astonishing seven more in a row before the Belgian GP. In a highly eventful race, the lead changed hands six times, and only 11 cars finished. Schumacher could only claim second place behind McLaren's Kimi Räikkönen, but the eight points were enough to propel the German legend to yet another World Championship, with four races still to be run. It was his seventh title in all, an unprecedented feat in Formula One.

▼ *Michael Schumacher corners his Ferrari F2004 at full speed during the 2004 Belgian GP, on the way to a seventh drivers' crown—and fifth in a row. The Italian team dominated the season, winning the constructors' title by a remarkable 143 points.*

U.S. RACING

As far as records show, the first race to be run in the U.S. was held on Thanksgiving Day, 1895. In ice and snow, Charles Duryea (the builder of one of America's first-ever motor vehicles in 1893) won at an average speed of 7.5mph (12km/h). Today's Indy Racing League and Champ Cars regularly clock speeds of more than 30 times that, while in 2005, one of the stars of the National Hot Rod Association (NHRA), Tony "The Sarge" Schumacher notched a Top Fuel dragster record of more than 336mph (543km/h).

Although there is a significant crossover in some of the major competitions, American racing has developed separately from racing in Europe, partially due to the legacy of the great distances between the two continents. An American, though, was responsible for one of Europe's first major competitions the Gordon Bennett Trophy, which is considered to be the forerunner of Grand Prix, while America's first great competition, the Vanderbilt Cup, ran from 1904 to 1916. In the same year that it ended, another competition began at Pikes Peak. The Pikes Peak International Hill Climb continues to this day and is the world's most famous hill climb event. Pioneering American racing was responsible for a number of world firsts, including the first-ever 24 hour race, which took place in Columbus, Ohio in 1905, and the first great oval track competition, the mighty Indianapolis 500. First raced in 1911, the Indy 500 is now a national fixture, despite the feud and split in IndyCar racing from the mid 1990s on, which saw the formation of the Indy Racing League (IRL), the collapse of CART, and the founding of the Champ Car World Series. Although rivaled by NASCAR's biggest race, the Daytona 500, the Indy 500 remains one of the greatest prizes in motorsports and has generated many outstanding records. A. J. Foyt's 35 starts and 13 races led, Al Unser's 644 laps led, and oldest winner at the age of 47, Eddie Cheever's fastest-ever race lap of 236.103mph (382km/h) in the 1996 race are among the most notable.

American racing today is extraordinarily varied and incredibly widespread. Many forms of racing are found in each state—from local motocross and sprint cars on oval tracks to Indy and Champ Car action and the thousands of events for amateurs and professionals organized by the American Motorcyclists Association (AMA). Formed in 1924, the AMA is largest national motorcycling association in the world, and its Pro Racing division was formed in 1994. It is responsible for six classes of motorcycle racing: Superbikes, Flat Track, Motocross, Hill Climb, Supercross, and Supermoto—a cross between road racing and motocross.

While Supercross is American motorcycle racing's biggest draw, NASCAR is, without question, American racing's biggest and most popular motorsports competition. NASCAR boasts phenomenal viewing figures and sell-out attendances at almost all of its 36 points-scoring races held during a season. It has spawned imitators, including CASCAR in Canada, AUSCAR in Australia, as well as the International Race of Champions (IROC) series—an invitation-only stock-car championship for leading NASCAR drivers, as well as racers from other classes such as Sprint car legend, Steve Kinser, Grand-Am stars like Max Papis and Wayne Taylor, and Indycar's Sam Hornish, Jr.

U.S. FACTS AND FIGURES

NACSAR CHAMPIONS

NASCAR's top competition was known as "Strictly Stock" in 1949, Grand National (1950–1971), the Winston Cup (1972–2003), and, since then, the Nextel Cup.

Year	Driver	Vehicle
2005	Tony Stewart	Chevrolet
2004	Kurt Busch	Ford
2003	Matt Kenseth	Ford
2002	Tony Stewart	Pontiac
2001	Jeff Gordon	Chevrolet
2000	Bobby Labonte	Pontiac
1999	Dale Jarrett	Ford
1998	Jeff Gordon	Chevrolet
1997	Jeff Gordon	Chevrolet
1996	Terry Labonte	Chevrolet
1995	Jeff Gordon	Chevrolet
1994	Dale Earnhardt	Chevrolet
1993	Dale Earnhardt	Chevrolet
1992	Alan Kulwicki	Ford
1991	Dale Earnhardt	Chevrolet
1990	Dale Earnhardt	Chevrolet
1989	Rusty Wallace	Pontiac
1988	Bill Elliot	Ford
1987	Dale Earnhardt	Chevrolet
1986	Dale Earnhardt	Chevrolet
1985	Darrell Waltrip	Chevrolet
1984	Terry Labonte	Chevrolet
1983	Bobby Allison	Buick
1982	Darrell Waltrip	Buick
1981	Darrell Waltrip	Buick
1980	Dale Earnhardt	Chevrolet
1979	Richard Petty	Chevrolet
1978	Cale Yarborough	Oldsmobile
1977	Cale Yarborough	Chevrolet
1976	Cale Yarborough	Chevrolet
1975	Richard Petty	Dodge
1974	Richard Petty	Dodge
1973	Benny Parsons	Chevrolet
1972	Richard Petty	Plymouth
1971	Richard Petty	Plymouth
1970	Bobby Isaac	Dodge

Year	Driver	Make
1969	David Pearson	Ford
1968	David Pearson	Ford
1967	Richard Petty	Plymouth
1966	David Pearson	Dodge
1965	Ned Jarrett	Ford
1964	Richard Petty	Plymouth
1963	Joe Weatherly	Pontiac
1962	Joe Weatherly	Pontiac
1961	Ned Jarrett	Chevrolet
1960	Rex White	Chevrolet
1959	Lee Petty	Plymouth
1958	Lee Petty	Oldsmobile
1957	Buck Baker	Chevrolet
1956	Buck Baker	Chrysler
1955	Tim Flock	Chrysler
1954	Lee Petty	Chrysler
1953	Herb Thomas	Hudson
1952	Tim Flock	Hudson
1951	Herb Thomas	Hudson
1950	Bill Rexford	Oldsmobile
1949	Red Byron	Oldsmobile

NACSAR Busch Series champions

Year	Driver	Make/Model
2005	Martin Truex, Jr.	Chevrolet
2004	Martin Truex, Jr.	Chevrolet
2003	Brian Vickers	Chevrolet
2002	Greg Biffle	Ford
2001	Kevin Harvick	Chevrolet
2000	Jeff Green	Chevrolet
1999	Dale Earnhardt, Jr.	Chevrolet
1998	Dale Earnhardt, Jr.	Chevrolet
1997	Randy LaJoie	Chevrolet
1996	Randy LaJoie	Chevrolet
1995	Johnny Benson	Chevrolet
1994	David Green	Chevrolet
1993	Steve Grissom	Chevrolet
1992	Joe Nemechek	Chevrolet
1991	Bobby Labonte	Oldsmobile
1990	Chuck Bown	Pontiac
1989	Rob Moroso	Oldsmobile
1988	Tommy Ellis	Buick
1987	Larry Pearson	Chevrolet
1986	Larry Pearson	Pontiac
1985	Jack Ingram	Pontiac
1984	Sam Ard	Oldsmobile
1983	Sam Ard	Oldsmobile
1982	Jack Ingram	Pontiac

NACSAR Craftsman Truck champions

Year	Driver	Make
2005	Ted Musgrave	Dodge
2004	Bobby Hamilton	Dodge
2003	Travis Kvapil	Chevrolet
2002	Mike Bliss	Chevrolet
2001	Jack Sprague	Chevrolet
2000	Greg Biffle	Ford
1999	Jack Sprague	Chevrolet
1998	Ron Hornaday	Chevrolet
1997	Jack Sprague	Chevrolet
1996	Ron Hornaday	Chevrolet
1995	Mike Skinner	Chevrolet

Indy 500 Race Champions

Year	Driver	Average speed (mph)
2005	Dan Wheldon	157.603
2004	Buddy Rice	138.518
2003	Gil de Ferran	156.291
2002	Helio Castroneves	166.499
2001	Helio Castroneves	153.601
2000	Juan Montoya	167.496
1999	Kenny Brack	153.176
1998	Eddie Cheever, Jr.	145.155
1997	Arie Luyendyk	145.827
1996	Buddy Lazier	147.956
1995	Jacques Villeneuve	153.616
1994	Al Unser, Jr.	160.872
1993	Emerson Fittipaldi	157.207
1992	Al Unser, Jr.	134.477
1991	Rick Mears	176.457
1990	Arie Luyendyk	185.981
1989	Emerson Fittipaldi	167.581
1988	Rick Mears	144.809
1987	Al Unser	162.175
1986	Bobby Rahal	170.722
1985	Danny Sullivan	152.982
1984	Rick Mears	163.612
1983	Tom Sneva	162.117
1982	Gordon Johncock	162.029
1981	Bobby Unser	139.084
1980	Johnny Rutherford	142.682
1979	Rick Mears	158.899
1978	Al Unser	161.363
1977	A. J. Foyt, Jr.	161.331
1976	Johnny Rutherford	148.725
1975	Bobby Unser	148.725
1974	Johnny Rutherford	158.589
1973	Gordon Johncock	159.036
1972	Mark Donohue	162.962
1971	Al Unser	157.735
1970	Al Unser	155.749
1969	Mario Andretti	156.867
1968	Bobby Unser	152.882
1967	A. J. Foyt, Jr.	151.207
1966	Graham Hill	144.317
1965	Jim Clark	150.686
1964	A. J. Foyt, Jr.	147.350
1963	Parnelli Jones	143.137
1962	Rodger Ward	140.293
1961	A. J. Foyt, Jr.	139.130
1960	Jim Rathmann	138.767
1959	Rodger Ward	135.857
1958	Jimmy Bryan	133.791
1957	Sam Hanks	135.601
1956	Pat Flaherty	128.490
1955	Bob Sweikert	128.213
1954	Bill Vukovich	130.840
1953	Bill Vukovich	128.740
1952	Troy Ruttman	128.922
1951	Lee Wallard	126.244
1950	Johnnie Parsons	124.002
1949	Bill Holland	121.327
1948	Mauri Rose	119.814
1947	Mauri Rose	116.338
1946	George Robson	114.820
1941	Floyd Davis	115.117
	Mauri Rose	115.117
1940	Wilbur Shaw	114.277
1939	Wilbur Shaw	115.035
1938	Floyd Roberts	117.200
1937	Wilbur Shaw	113.580
1936	Lou Meyer	109.069
1935	Kelly Petillo	106.240
1934	Bill Cummings	104.863
1933	Lou Meyer	104.162
1932	Fred Frame	104.144
1931	Louis Schneider	96.629
1930	Billy Arnold	100.448
1929	Ray Keech	97.585
1928	Lou Meyer	99.482

1927	George Souders	97.545
1926	Frank Lockhart	95.904
1925	Peter DePaolo	101.127
1924	L. L. Corum	98.234
	Joe Boyer	98.234
1923	Tommy Milton	90.954
1922	Jimmy Murphy	94.484
1921	Tommy Milton	89.621
1920	Gaston Chevrolet	88.618
1919	Howdy Wilcox	88.050
1916	Dario Resta	84.001
1915	Ralph DePalma	89.840
1914	Rene Thomas	82.474
1913	Jules Goux	75.933
1912	Joe Dawson	78.719
1911	Ray Harroun	74.602

INDY RACING LEAGUE (IRL) CHAMPIONS

Year	Driver	Team
2005	Dan Wheldon (U.K.)	Andretti-Green
2004	Tony Kanaan (Brazil)	Andretti-Green
2003	Scott Dixon (New Zealand)	Ganassi
2002	Sam Hornish, Jr. (U.S.)	Panther Racing
2001	Sam Hornish, Jr. (U.S.)	Panther Racing
2000	Buddy Lazier (U.S.)	Hemelgarn Racing
1999	Greg Ray (U.S.)	Team Menard
1998	Kenny Brack (Sweden)	A. J. Foyt Racing
1996	Tony Stewart (U.S)	Team Menard
1997	Tony Stewart (U.S)	Team Menard
1996	Buzz Calkins (U.S)	Bradley Motorsports
	Scott Sharp (U.S)	A. J. Foyt Racing

CART/CHAMP CAR CHAMPIONS

Year	Driver	Team
2005	Sebastien Bourdais (France)	Newman-Haas
2004	Sebastien Bourdais (France)	Newman-Haas
2003	Paul Tracy (Canada)	Forsythe
2002	Cristiano da Matta (Brazil)	Newman-Haas
2001	Gil de Ferran (Brazil)	Penske
2000	Gil de Ferran (Brazil)	Penske
1999	Juan Pablo Montoya (Colombia)	Ganassi
1998	Alex Zanardi (Italy)	Ganassi
1997	Alex Zanardi (Italy)	Ganassi
1996	Jimmy Vasser (U.S.)	Ganassi
1995	Jacques Villeneuve (Canada)	Green
1994	Al Unser, Jr. (U.S.)	Penske
1993	Nigel Mansell (U.K.)	Newman-Haas
1992	Bobby Rahal (U.S.)	Rahal-Hogan
1991	Michael Andretti (U.S.)	Newman-Haas
1990	Al Unser, Jr. (U.S.)	Galles-Kraco
1989	Emerson Fittipaldi (Brazil)	Patrick
1988	Danny Sullivan (U.S.)	Penske
1987	Bobby Rahal (U.S.)	Truesports
1986	Bobby Rahal (U.S.)	Truesports
1985	Al Unser, Sr. (U.S.)	Penske
1984	Mario Andretti (U.S.)	Newman-Haas
1983	Al Unser, Sr. (U.S.)	Penske
1982	Rick Mears (U.S.)	Penske
1981	Rick Mears (U.S.)	Penske
1980	Johnny Rutherford (U.S.)	Chaparral
1979	Rick Mears (U.S.)	Penske

FORMULA ONE WORLD CHAMPIONS

Second teams listed in brackets were constructors champions but did not provide the car of the winning driver.

Year	Driver	Driver's Team
2005	Fernando Alonso (Spain)	Renault
2004	Michael Schumacher (Germany)	Ferrari
2003	Michael Schumacher (Germany)	Ferrari
2002	Michael Schumacher (Germany)	Ferrari
2001	Michael Schumacher (Germany)	Ferrari
2000	Michael Schumacher (Germany)	Ferrari
1999	Mika Hakkinen (Finland)	McLaren-Mercedes (Ferrari)
1998	Mika Hakkinen (Finland)	McLaren-Mercedes
1997	Jacques Villeneuve (Canada)	Williams-Renault
1996	Damon Hill (U.K.)	Williams-Renault
1995	Michael Schumacher (Germany)	Benetton-Renault
1994	Michael Schumacher (Germany)	Benetton-Ford (Williams-Renault)
1993	Alain Prost (France)	Williams-Renault
1992	Nigel Mansell (U.K.)	Williams-Renault
1991	Ayrton Senna (Brazil)	McLaren-Honda
1990	Ayrton Senna (Brazil)	McLaren-Honda
1989	Alain Prost (France)	McLaren-Honda
1988	Ayrton Senna (Brazil)	McLaren-Honda
1987	Nelson Piquet (Brazil)	Williams-Honda
1986	Alain Prost (France)	McLaren-TAG Porsche (Williams-Honda)
1985	Alain Prost (France)	McLaren-TAG Porsche
1984	Niki Lauda (Austria)	McLaren-TAG Porsche
1983	Nelson Piquet (Brazil)	Brabham-BMW (Ferrari)
1982	Keke Rosberg (Finland)	Williams-Ford (Ferrari)
1981	Nelson Piquet (Brazil)	Brabham-Ford
1980	Alan Jones (Australia)	Williams-Ford
1979	Jody Scheckter (South Africa)	Ferrari
1978	Mario Andretti (U.S.)	Lotus-Ford
1977	Niki Lauda (Austria)	Ferrari
1976	James Hunt (England)	McLaren-Ford (Ferrari)
1975	Niki Lauda (Austria)	Ferrari
1974	Emerson Fittipaldi (Brazil)	McLaren-Ford
1973	Jackie Stewart (Scotland)	Tyrell-Ford (Lotus Ford)
1972	Emerson Fittipaldi (Brazil)	Lotus-Ford
1971	Jackie Stewart (Scotland)	Tyrell-Ford
1970	Jochen Rindt (Austria)	Lotus-Ford
1969	Jackie Stewart (Scotland)	Matra-Ford
1968	Graham Hill (U.K.)	Lotus-Ford
1967	Denis Hulme (New Zealand)	Brabham-Repco
1966	Jack Brabham (Australia)	Brabham-Repco
1965	Jim Clark (Scotland)	Lotus-Climax
1964	John Surtees (U.K.)	Ferrari
1963	Jim Clark (Scotland)	Lotus-Climax
1962	Graham Hill (U.K.)	BRM
1961	Phil Hill (U.S.)	Ferrari
1960	Jack Brabham (Australia)	Cooper-Climax
1959	Jack Brabham (Australia)	Cooper-Climax
1958	Mike Hawthorn (U.K.)	Ferrari (Vanwall)
1957	Juan-Manuel Fangio (Argentina)	Maserati
1956	Juan-Manuel Fangio (Argentina)	Ferrari
1955	Juan-Manuel Fangio (Argentina)	Mercedes
1954	Juan-Manuel Fangio (Argentina)	Maserati/Mercedes
1953	Alberto Ascari (Italy)	Ferrari
1952	Alberto Ascari (Italy)	Ferrari
1951	Juan-Manuel Fangio (Argentina)	Alfa Romeo
1950	Guiseppe Farina (Italy)	Alfa Romeo

GP500 AND MotoGP CHAMPIONS

Year	Rider	Team
2005	Valentino Rossi (Italy)	Yamaha
2004	Valentino Rossi (Italy)	Yamaha
2003	Valentino Rossi (Italy)	Honda
2002	Valentino Rossi (Italy)	Honda
2001	Valentino Rossi (Italy)	Honda
2000	Kenny Roberts, Jr. (U.S.)	Suzuki
1999	Alex Criville (Spain)	Honda
1998	Mick Doohan (Australia)	Honda
1997	Mick Doohan (Australia)	Honda
1996	Mick Doohan (Australia)	Honda

1995	Mick Doohan (Australia)	Honda
1994	Mick Doohan (Australia)	Honda
1993	Kevin Schwantz (U.S.)	Suzuki
1992	Wayne Rainey (U.S.)	Yamaha
1991	Wayne Rainey (U.S.)	Yamaha
1990	Wayne Rainey (U.S.)	Yamaha
1989	Eddie Lawson (U.S.)	Honda
1988	Eddie Lawson (U.S.)	Yamaha
1987	Wayne Gardner (Australia)	Honda
1986	Eddie Lawson (U.S.)	Yamaha
1985	Freddie Spencer (U.S.)	Honda
1984	Eddie Lawson (U.S.)	Yamaha
1983	Freddie Spencer (U.S.)	Honda
1982	Franco Uncini (Italy)	Suzuki
1981	Marco Lucchinelli (Italy)	Suzuki
1980	Kenny Roberts (U.S.)	Yamaha
1979	Kenny Roberts (U.S.)	Yamaha
1978	Kenny Roberts (U.S.)	Yamaha
1977	Barry Sheene (U.K.)	Suzuki
1976	Barry Sheene (U.K.)	Suzuki
1975	Giacomo Agostini (Italy)	Yamaha
1974	Phil Read (U.K.)	MV Agusta
1973	Phil Read (U.K.)	MV Agusta
1972	Giacomo Agostini (Italy)	MV Agusta
1971	Giacomo Agostini (Italy)	MV Agusta
1970	Giacomo Agostini (Italy)	MV Agusta
1969	Giacomo Agostini (Italy)	MV Agusta
1968	Giacomo Agostini (Italy)	MV Agusta
1967	Giacomo Agostini (Italy)	MV Agusta
1966	Giacomo Agostini (Italy)	MV Agusta
1965	Mike Hailwood (U.K.)	MV Agusta
1964	Mike Hailwood (U.K.)	MV Agusta
1963	Mike Hailwood (U.K.)	MV Agusta
1962	Mike Hailwood (U.K.)	MV Agusta
1961	Gary Hocking (U.K.)	MV Agusta
1960	John Surtees (U.K.)	MV Agusta
1959	John Surtees (U.K.)	MV Agusta
1958	John Surtees (U.K.)	MV Agusta
1957	Libero Liberati (Italy)	Gilera
1956	John Surtees (U.K.)	MV Agusta
1955	Geoff Duke (U.K.)	Gilera
1954	Geoff Duke (U.K.)	Gilera
1953	Geoff Duke (U.K.)	Gilera
1952	Umberto Masetti (Italy)	Gilera
1951	Geoff Duke (U.K.)	Norton
1950	Umberto Masetti (Italy)	Gilera
1949	Leslie Graham (U.K.)	AJS

AMA SUPERCROSS 250CC CHAMPIONS

Year	Rider	Team
2005	Ricky Carmichael	Suzuki
2004	Chad Reed	Yamaha
2003	Ricky Carmichael	Honda
2002	Ricky Carmichael	Honda
2001	Ricky Carmichael	Kawasaki
2000	Jeremy McGrath	Yamaha
1999	Jeremy McGrath	Yamaha
1998	Jeremy McGrath	Yamaha
1997	Jeff Emig	Kawasaki
1996	Jeremy McGrath	Honda
1995	Jeremy McGrath	Honda
1994	Jeremy McGrath	Honda
1993	Jeremy McGrath	Honda
1992	Jeff Stanton	Honda
1991	Jean-Michel Bayles	Honda
1990	Jeff Stanton	Honda
1989	Jeff Stanton	Honda
1988	Rick Johnson	Honda
1987	Jeff Ward	Kawasaki
1986	Rick Johnson	Honda

1985	Jeff Ward	Kawasaki
1984	Johnny O'Mara	Honda
1983	David Bailey	Honda
1982	Donnie Hansen	Honda
1981	Mark Barnett	Suzuki
1980	Mike Bell	Yamaha
1979	Bob Hannah	Yamaha
1978	Bob Hannah	Yamaha
1977	Bob Hannah	Yamaha
1976	Jim Weinert	Kawasaki
1975	Jim Ellis	Can-Am
1974	Pierre Karsmakers	Yamaha

AMA SUPERBIKE CHAMPIONS

Year	Rider	Team
2005	Matt Mladin	Suzuki
2004	Matt Mladin	Suzuki
2003	Matt Mladin	Suzuki
2002	Nicky Hayden	Honda
2001	Matt Mladin	Suzuki
2000	Matt Mladin	Suzuki
1999	Matt Mladin	Suzuki
1998	Ben Bostrom	Honda
1997	Doug Chandler	Kawasaki
1996	Doug Chandler	Kawasaki
1995	Miguel Duhamel	Honda
1994	Troy Corser	Ducati
1993	Doug Polen	Ducati
1992	Scott Russell	Kawasaki
1991	Thomas Stevens	Yamaha
1990	Doug Chandler	Kawasaki
1989	Jamie James	Suzuki
1988	Bubba Shobert	Honda
1987	Wayne Rainey	Honda
1986	Fred Merkel	Honda
1985	Fred Merkel	Honda
1984	Fred Merkel	Honda
1983	Wayne Rainey	Kawasaki
1982	Eddie Lawson	Kawasaki
1981	Eddie Lawson	Kawasaki
1980	Wes Cooley	Suzuki
1979	Wes Cooley	Suzuki
1978	Reg Pridmore	Kawasaki
1977	Reg Pridmore	Kawasaki
1976	Reg Pridmore	BMW

WORLD SUPERBIKE CHAMPIONS

Year	Rider	Team
2005	Troy Corser (Australia)	Suzuki
2004	James Toseland (U.K.)	Ducati
2003	Neil Hodgson (U.K.)	Ducati
2002	Colin Edwards (U.S.)	Honda
2001	Troy Bayliss (Australia)	Ducati
2000	Colin Edwards (U.S.)	Honda
1999	Carl Fogarty (U.K.)	Ducati
1998	Carl Fogarty (U.K.)	Ducati
1997	John Kocinski (U.S.)	Honda
1996	Troy Corser (Australia)	Ducati
1995	Carl Fogarty (U.K.)	Ducati
1994	Carl Fogarty (U.K.)	Ducati
1993	Scott Russell (U.S.)	Kawasaki
1992	Doug Polen (U.S.)	Ducati
1991	Doug Polen (U.S.)	Ducati
1990	Raymond Roche (France)	Ducati
1989	Fred Merkel (U.S.)	Honda
1988	Fred Merkel (U.S.)	Honda

Aerodynamics In motor racing, the science and study of how air flows over, under, and around a race vehicle as it moves.

AMA The American Motorcyclist Association—the body that organizes and promotes the leading motorcycle racing competitions in the U.S.

Apex The part of a turn, usually the slowest point, where the car is closest to the inside edge of the track.

Apron The paved inside edge of many tracks that separates the racing surface from the infield.

Banking The sloping of the track surface, especially the bends, that is measured in degrees from the horizontal.

Burnout The spinning of the rear tires in drag racing to heat them up before a race so that they reach their ideal operating temperature.

Carbon fiber A material originally developed for the aerospace industry that is exceptionally light and strong and is used for the chassis and other body parts of many race vehicles.

Caution A period of a race when the competitors have to slow down due to an accident or some other problem on the track.

Chassis The basic frame or structure of a race car, to which all other components are attached.

Chicane A combination of corners which go one way and then the other, usually found on a straight, and designed to slow down vehicles.

Displacement The size of an engine in cubic centimeters (cc) or liters. It is sometimes referred to as engine capacity.

Downforce A force caused by the way that air flows around a car. It helps push the car down onto the racing surface.

Drafting The driver's use of the car ahead to reduce their own vehicle's wind resistance and gain additional speed or maintain speed, using less engine power. Also known as slipstreaming.

Drag The resistance that a vehicle experiences when it moves through the air. This force slows a vehicle down, and the amount of force increases with speed. Vehicles are designed to cut through the air as smoothly as possible to create less drag.

Drift A controlled sideways slide through a turn, sometimes used to get the nose of the car pointing in the best racing line out of the corner.

Elapsed time (ET) The time that it takes a vehicle to travel from the starting line to the finish line—a particularly important measurement used in drag racing.

Esses A series of sharp right and left turns on a circuit.

FIA The *Fédération Internationale de l'Automobile*—the organization that oversees many of motorsports' biggest competitions.

FIM The *Fédération Internationale de Motocyclisme*—the body that organizes many of the world's premier motorcycling events.

Grip The ability of a car or motorcycle, its suspension, aerodynamics, and tires to hold the car to the road, while transmitting the power of the engine into forward movement.

Ground effect A phenomenon that occurs as air moves beneath a vehicle, creating an area of low pressure and helping the vehicle "stick" to the ground.

Hairpin A very tight and slow corner that usually takes a car through a 180° change of direction.

Handling How a car responds when it is racing, particularly to changes in speed and direction. A car's design, construction, and the choice and settings of its body, aerodynamics, tires, and suspension can all have major effects on its handling.

Horsepower (hp) A unit of measurement that indicates the amount of power that an engine generates. A family car may generate 70–120 horsepower, while a Formula One car engine may generate more than 750 horsepower.

IndyCar A term used today for the cars that compete in the Indy Racing League (IRL). In the past, it was used to describe open-wheel vehicles that competed in American Championship car racing.

Lead lap The lap of the track that the race leader is currently on.

Monocoque An all-in-one vehicle body design where the outer skin supports most of the vehicle's weight instead of an internal frame.

NASCAR National Association for Stock Car Auto Racing, the organizing body of NASCAR racing, founded in 1948.

Oversteer A situation in which the front of the car grips the racing surface, but the back end loses grip and may start to slide out.

Paddock The area at a race track that includes the garages, inspection areas, hospitality areas, media center, and drivers' and officials' trailers.

Parc fermé The area where competitors in rallying and some other classes of racing are required to park their race vehicles, which then cannot be modified until they are released from the area.

Pit lane The separate road that runs inside of the race circuit, where vehicles go for a pit stop for fresh tires and fuel and to have running repairs made.

Podium place A top-three finish in a race, so called because the top three finishers stand on a podium to receive their trophies or medals.

Pole position In many classes, this is the best position at the front of the starting grid. It is given to the vehicle that qualifies with the fastest time.

Pole winner The driver who gains pole position at a race.

Qualifying Sessions or actual races that determine the entries and order on the starting grid of a major race.

Racing line The optimum route around a circuit or race route, in particular the precise line that is taken by vehicles through the corners.

Revs Short for revolutions per minute (rpm), used to measure the speed at which a vehicle's engine operates.

Roll cage The tubular steel frame inside of a car designed to protect the driver (and codriver) in a crash.

Run-off area Part of a circuit designed to allow cars and bikes that leave the track to come to a halt safely, avoiding a serious accident.

Setup The preparation of a race vehicle before qualifying or a race. It includes the choice of suspension, tire type and pressure, gearing, and engine tuning.

Shock absorbers Devices that are designed to absorb sudden forces and impacts to the suspension of the vehicle. Also known as shocks.

Slick A type of tire with a smooth outer surface and no tread grooves, used in some classes of racing on dry tracks.

Slingshot An overtaking move in which one car drafts behind another and then pulls out, using its momentum to pass its rival.

Special stage A competitive part of a rally such as those in the World Rally Championship. It is a section timed to fractions of a second, which a rally team must complete as quickly as possible.

Spoiler An aerodynamic device designed to create air turbulence, which helps cause downforce.

Starting grid The area of the track where the vehicles line up just before a race starts, in order of their qualifying times.

Super special stage A stage of a rally, often run in a stadium, that features two cars competing side by side on courses of identical length and design.

Superspeedway A long, oval track. In NASCAR, cars racing on superspeedways have restrictor plates attached to keep their speeds down to a safe level.

Suspension The system of springs, shock absorbers, and other components, directly connected to the wheels or the axles, that affects the handling of a race vehicle.

Telemetry A radio device that relays information (collected by electronic sensors) about the car's engine, tires, brakes, and other key components, back to the team's base as the car is running in testing or in a race.

Tire blanket Also known as a tire warmer, this is an electric heater that covers a new tire, keeping it warm at the trackside before it is fitted to the car during a pit stop.

Tire compound The exact blend of rubber and other substances that is used to achieve the best tire for a particular racing setup or in particular weather and track conditions.

Traction control A computer-controlled electronic system that helps prevent wheelspin and loss of grip, while delivering as much power to the wheels as the racer requires.

Transponder A radio transmitting device that is attached to some cars, which monitors lap times and speeds around a circuit.

Transporter The truck that moves all cars and their equipment from circuit to circuit.

Tri-oval A modified oval race track with an additional slight turn along one of its straights.

Understeer A vehicle handling phenomenon that occurs when the front wheels lose grip more than the rear. This tends to push the nose of the car out of a bend when cornering.

Victory lane A circle, square, or fenced-in area where a driver celebrates a winning finish with his or her family, team bosses, crew, and sponsors.

Wheelbase The distance between the front and rear axles of a car or motorcycle.

Window webbing Nylon net screens attached to the driver's window that help keep the driver inside of the car in an accident.

RESOURCES

WEB SITES

http://www.autoracing1.com
Excellent U.S. site with news and standings on major competitions, including NASCAR, F1, IRL, and Champ Cars.

http://whowon.com
Fantastic news Web site with many aspects of racing in North America, including drag racing, karting, and sprint and midget cars.

http://www.racingone.com Dedicated to all motorsports classes, featuring Grand-Am, World of Outlaws, and ARCA events.

www.nascar.com The official Web site of NASCAR racing is packed with stats, facts, news, and interviews with drivers and team bosses.

http://insidethegroove.com/index.php
A comprehensive collection of statistics for NASCAR racing.

http://www.atthetrackracing.com/
drivers/links.htm Handy links pages with directions to dozens of NASCAR and NHRA drivers' official Web sites.

www.indycar.com The official site of the Indy Racing League has the latest racing news, lots of free-to-view video clips, and excellent technical features.

http://www.champcarworldseries.com
/FrontPage.asp The official Web site of the Champ Car World Series, with plenty of data on the drivers, team, races, and standings.

www.formula1.com The official F1 Web site has large technical and rules sections, plus interactive maps of the circuits featured in the current season.

http://www.nhra.com The official Web site of the world's biggest drag racing organization, with race schedules and action photos.

http:www.nasarallysport.com
The official Web site of the National Auto Sport Association, which runs many rallies in the U.S.

http://www.rally-america.com
Informative Web site about the Rally American competition, including a glossary and rallying for beginners.

http://www.etracksonline.co.uk
Dedicated to the racing circuits of the world, this site can be searched by name, country, or continent, plus features on track design and engineers.

http://www.scca.org Internet home of the Sports Car Club of America, with details of their racing events.

http://www.thundervalleyracing.com
The Web site for women racers and race fans, with lots of great links for female drivers' Web sites.

http://www.americanlemans.com
The official ALMS site, with galleries of photos and features.

http://www.amaproracing.com
Home of the AMA's (American Motorcyclist Association) racing division. Providing links to Web sites for Superbikes, Motocross, Supercross, Hill Climb, Supermoto, and flat and dirt-track racing.

www.clivegifford.co.uk
The Web site for the author of this book, with dedicated Web pages and more links to great motorsports sites.

BOOKS AND MAGAZINES

American Auto Racing (James A. Martin and Thomas F. Saal, McFarland & Co., 2004) An excellent chronicle of racing in the U.S., plus major races and racers.

NASCAR for Dummies, 2nd edition (Mark Martin and Beth Tuschak, Wiley Publishing, 2005) Written by a major NASCAR star, this is an excellent guide to the rules, vehicles, drivers, and strategy of NASCAR.

Indy 500: The Inside Track (Nancy Roe Pimm, Darby Creek Publishing, 2004) A young person's guide to the Indy 500.

Pro Motocross and Off-Road Motorcycle Riding Techniques (Donnie Bales with Gary Semics, MBI Publishing, 2001) A thorough guide to the equipment and techniques used to ride motocross and off-road bikes in competitions and for fun.

American Drag Racing (Robert Genat, MBI Publishing, 2001) A great guide, full of photos from the NHRA archives, charting how drag racing has developed from the 1950s to the present.

NASCAR Pit Pass (Bob Woods, Reader's Digest, 2005) A behind-the-scenes guide to NASCAR written for young adults.

Racer magazine
Covering all aspects of motorsports, from ALMS and NASCAR to Indy and Champ Cars and drag racing.

Road Racer X magazine
A through guide to the exciting world of motorcycle road racing, covering AMA and other American series, as well as MotoGP and Superbike action.

Car and Driver magazine
Featuring new cars, technical features, and motor-racing events.

INDEX

Note: references to main entries are in **bold**.

ACKNOWLEDGMENTS

The publisher would like to thank the following for permission to reproduce their material. Every care has been taken to trace copyright holders. However, if there have been unintentional omissions or failure to trace copyright holders, we apologize and will, if informed, endeavor to make corrections in any future edition.

Top = t, bottom = b, center = c, left = l, right = r

Front cover Getty Images Sport/Paul Kane; back cover t LAT Photographic/Jeff Bloxham; back cover c Empics/AP/Igor Sefr; back cover b Corbis/ World Racing Images/Laurent Charniaux; page 1 Marcos Borga/Reuters/Corbis; 2–3 Schlegelmilch/Corbis; 4 Kinrade/Sutton; 5 Albert Gea/Reuters/Corbis; 6l China Photos/Reuters/Corbis, c Victor Tonelli/Reuters/Corbis, r Gero Breloer/EPA/Corbis; 7t Reuters/Corbis, b LAT Photographic; 8t National Motor Museum/MPL, b Topical Press Agency/Getty Images; 9l MPI/Getty Images, tr National Motor Museum/MPL, br Hulton Deutsch Collection/Corbis; 10l LAT Photographic, tr Hulton Deutsch Collection/Corbis, 10–11 S & G/Empics/Alpha, 11tr LAT Photographic, br Bettmann/Corbis; 12t Max Rossi/Reuters/Corbis, b Raoux John/Orlando Sentinel/Corbis Sygma; 13t Mark Horsburgh/Reuters/Corbis, c Jonathan Ferry/Getty Images, b Bert Hardy/Picture Post/Getty Images; 14–15 Sam Sharpe/Corbis, 15 (inset) Kinrade/Sutton; 16t Popperfoto/Sutton, b Jeff Bloxham/LAT Photographic; 17t Nick Laham/Getty Images, c & b Sutton; 18t Paul Mounce/Corbis, b Mike Powell/Getty Images; 19t USA LAT Photographic, bl Jamie Squire/Getty Images, br Greg Aleck LAT Photographic; 20t Moy/Sutton, c Sutton, b Schlegelmilch/Corbis; 21t Alexander Hassenstein/Bongarts/Getty Images, b Schlegelmilch/Corbis; 22t Sutton, b Yves Herman/Reuters/Corbis; 23t Jose Jordan/AFP/Getty Images, b Bryn Lennon/Getty Images; 24 Schlegelmilch/Corbis; 25t Andreas Rentz/Bongarts/Getty Images, c Phipps/Sutton, b Schlegelmilch/Corbis; 26t Gary Hawkins/LAT Photographic, c Ferraro/LAT, b Bumstead/Sutton; 27t & c Batchelor/LAT, b Hardwick/Sutton; 28 Darrell Ingham/Getty Images, 28–29 Harold Hinson/TSN/Zuma/Corbis, 29t Jamie Squire/Getty Images; 30t Sam Sharpe/Corbis, c Robert Lesieur/LAT Photographic, b George Tiedemann/Newsport/Corbis; 31t Sam Sharpe/Corbis, b Sutton; 33t Sam Sharpe/Corbis, b Jamie Squire/Getty Images; 33t Marc Serota/Reuters/Corbis, b Rusty Jarrett/Getty Images, b George Tiedemann/Newsport/Corbis; 34l Sutton, 34–35 Robert Cianflone/Getty Images, 35t Vladimir Rys/Bongarts/Getty Images, b Sutton; 36t Phipps/Sutton, c Sutton, b Dan Streck/USA,LAT Photographic; 37t Surget/Sutton, b Sutton; 38l Miroslav Zajic/Corbis, r Capilitan/Sutton, 38–39b World/Sutton, 39t Thorne/Sutton, c Popperfoto/Sutton; 40t Sutton, c Louisa Gouliamaki/AFP/Getty Images, b Hardwick/Sutton; 41t Grazia Neri/Allsport/Getty Images, c Hardwick/Sutton, b Jo Lillini/Corbis; 42t & cl Hardwick/Sutton, cr Carl de Souza/AFP/Getty Images, b Sutton; 43t Luis Acosta/AFP/Getty Images, b Prakash Singh/AFP/Getty Images; 44t Bryn Lennon/Getty Images, c Reuters/Corbis, b Eriko Sugita/Reuters/Corbis; 45t Mark Horsburgh/Reuters/Corbis, c Martin Philbey/EPA/Corbis, b James Taylor/Newsport/Corbis; 46t Pascal Rondeau/Allsport/Getty Images, c Pierre Tostee/Getty Images, b Jeff Kardas/Getty Images; 47t Gary M Prior/Allsport/Getty Images, b Reuters/Corbis; 48t Russell Batchelor/LAT Photographic, c F Pierce Williams/LAT Photographic, b Rose/LAT Photographic; 49t Bryn Lennon/Getty Images, bl Franck Fife/AFP/Getty Images, br Ken Sklute/AP/Empics; 50t Glen Dunbar/LAT Photographic, c David Zalubowski/AP/Empics, b Steve Etherington/LAT Photographic; 51t Jeff Bloxham/LAT Photographic, c Mauricio Lima/AFP/Getty Images, b Sutton; 52t Clive Mason/Allsport/Getty Images, c Peter Tarry/Action Plus, b Doug Pensinger/Getty Images; 53t Sutton, c Phil Cole/Allsport/Getty Images, b Duomo/Corbis; 54–55 Sutton, 55t (inset) Photo4/LAT Photographic, b (inset) Jonathan Ferry/Getty Images; 56l Paul A Souders/Corbis, r LAT Photographic; 57 Schlegelmilch/Corbis; 58t Topical Press Agency/Getty Images, bl National Motor Museum/MPL, br Sutton; 59tl Peter Spinney/LAT Photographic, tr Dan R. Boyd/USA, LAT Photographic, b Schlegelmilch/Corbis; 60t John Gress/Reuters/Corbis, bl Toyota F1 Racing/Sutton, 60–61 Jay Sailors/AP/Empics, 61t George D. Lepp/Corbis; 62t Yoshikazu Tsuno/AFP/Getty Images, c Moy/Sutton, b Damien Meyer/AFP/Getty Images; 63t Reuters/Corbis, b Schlegelmilch/Corbis; 64t LAT Photographic, b William West/AFP/Getty Images, 64–65 Kimimasa Mayama/Reuters/Corbis, 65t Tim Tadder/Newsport/Corbis; 66t Robert LeSieur/LAT Photographic, b Moy/Sutton; 67t Robert LeSieur/USA, LAT Photographic, c Klynsmith/Sutton, b Sutton;

68 West/Sutton; 69t Jon Ferrey/Allsport/Getty Images, c LAT Photographic, b Harwick/Sutton; 70t Lesley Ann Miller,USA LAT Photographic, b Adrian Dennis/AFP/Getty Images; 71t Bearne/Sutton, b Kazuhiro Nogi/AFP/Getty Images; 72–73 Sutton; 74t Kazuhiro Nogi/AFP/Getty Images, c & b LAT Photographic; 75t Michael Kim/Corbis, b Bryn Lennon/Getty Images; 76l Sutton, r Patrick Hertzog/AFP/Getty Images; 77t Schlegelmilch/Corbis, b Stefano Rellandini/Reuters/Corbis; 78t National Motor Museum/MPL, b Richard Dole/USA LAT Photographic; 79t Hardwick/Sutton, b Brian Bahr/Allsport/Getty Images; 80t Clive Mason/Getty Images, c Pascal Rondeau/Getty Images, b Martin Bureau/AFP/Getty Images; 81t Mark Thompson/Allsport/Getty Images, b Vern Fisher/AP/Empics; 82t Damien Meyer/AFP/Getty Images, c Jakob Ebrey/LAT Photographic, b Icon SMI/Corbis; 83t Mark Horsburgh/LAT Photographic, b David Lees/Corbis; 84–85 LAT Photographic; 86t Sutton, b Malcolm Griffiths/LAT Photographic, 86–87 Sutton, 87 c & b Capilitan/Sutton; 88t Jed Leicester/Empics, cl DPPI/LAT Photographic, cr LAT Photographic, b Emeric De Bare/World Racing Images/Corbis; 89t Moy/Sutton, c Steve Etherington/LAT Photographic, b Jo Lillini/Corbis; 90t Darrell Ingham/Getty Images, b Jo Lillini/Corbis; 91t Clive Rose/JPR/Getty Images, b Gero Breloer/DPA/Empics; 92t DPA/Empics, b Ron Heflin/AP/Empics; 93t Joe Klamar/AFP/Getty Images, b Tingle/LAT Photographic; 94t Sutton, b Lesley Ann Miller/USA LAT Photographic; 95tl Bryn Lennon/Allsport/Getty images, tr Toshifumi Kitamura/AFP/Getty Images, c Robert LeSieur USA/LAT Photographic, b Steve Etherington/LAT Photographic; 96t Clive Rose/Getty Images, c Carlos Barria/Reuters/Corbis, b Steve Etherington/LAT Photographic, 96–97 Clive Rose/Getty Images; 98t Paul Gilham/Getty Images, c Central Press/Getty Images, b LAT Photographic; 99t Ross Land/Getty Images, c (main image) Larry Kasperek/Newsport/ Corbis, b Lynne Sladky/AP/Empics; 100t Duomo/Corbis, c J Hardman/Fox Photos/Getty Images, b Cameron Spencer/Getty Images; 101t Martin Cleaver/AP/Empics, b Brent Smith/Reuters/Corbis; 102 tl George Olson/Time Life Pictures/Getty Images, tr LAT Photography, b Javier Soriano/AFP/Getty Images; 103t Michael Cooper/Allsport/Getty Images, b LAT Photographic; 104t Mike Cooper/Allsport/Getty Images, cl Allsport/Hulton Archive/Getty images, cr Patrick Hertzog/AFP/Getty Images, 104–105 Simon Bruty/Allsport/Getty Images, 105l Bettmann/Corbis, r Schlegelmilch/Corbis; 106t LAT Photographic, 106–107 Robert Cianflone/Getty Images, 107tr LAT Photographic, br AP/Empics; tl LAT Photography bl Schlegelmilch/Corbis, 108tl LAT Photography, bl Schlegelmilch/Corbis, r Tod Panagopoulos/AFP/Getty Images; 109t Brent Smith/Reuters/Corbis, b Allsport/Getty Images; 110tl Nicolas Asfouri/AFP/Getty Images, tr Bettmann/Corbis, b Schlegelmilch/Corbis; 111t Allsport/Getty Images, b Ian Walton/Allsport/Getty Images; 112tl Mark Thompson/Allsport/Getty Images, tr & b LAT Photographic; 113t Bettmann/Corbis, b Hulton Archive/Getty Images; 114t Robert Laberge/Getty Images, b Keystone/Getty Images; 115t Anton Want/Allsport/Getty Images, bl Victor Blackman/Express/Getty Images, br LAT Photographic; 116t Philippe Desmazes/AFP/Getty Images, b S & G Empics; 117t Steve Powell/Allsport/ Getty Images, c Mureenbeeld/LAT Photographic, b Vittoriano Rastelli/Corbis; 118–119 Paul Mounce/ Corbis, 119t USA LAT Photographic; 120t Murenbeeld/LAT Photographic, b Ben Wood/Corbis; 121t LAT Photographic, c Reporter Images/ Getty Images, b Robert Laberge/Getty Images; 122tl Ronald Startup/ Getty Images, tr USA LAT Photographic, 122–123 Don Heiny/Corbis, 123l Mike Cooper/ Allsport/Getty Images, r Paul/Sutton; 124t Stringer/USA/Reuters/Corbis, cl Darrell Ingham/Getty Images, bl Reuters/ Corbis, r Mark Horsburgh/Reuters/Corbis; 125 Schlegelmilch/Corbis; 126tl National Motor Museum/MPL, tr Schlegelmilch/Corbis, b Phipps/Sutton; 127t Express Newspapers/Getty, b Hawkins/Sutton; 128t Dave Friedman/LAT Photographic, c LAT Photographic, b David Allio/Icon SMI/Corbis; 129l Bernard Cahier/The Cahier Archive, tr Phipps/Sutton, bl National Motor Museum/MPL, br Schlegelmilch/Corbis; 130t McNeil/Sutton, b Moy/Sutton; 131t Andrew Wong/Getty Images, c Moy/Sutton, b Bettmann/Corbis; 132–133 Pascal Rossignol/Reuters/Corbis; *Poster*: Main image: Sutton Motorsports/Patching; From left to right: Getty Images Sport / Clive Mason; Sutton Motorsports;Sutton Motorsports/Capilitan; Corbis/Schlegelmilch; Empics/AP/Ron Heflin

The publisher would also like to thank James Mossop and *The Sunday Telegraph* for permission to reprint figures from the article "Top teams no longer have money to burn" (February 29, 2004) regarding the cost of components for the Jaguar R5 Formula One car (see pages 88–89).